Happy Days with SNOOPY

- A Basic English Handbook -

by Hidehiko Konaka

Asahi Press

PEANUTS Characters

Charlie Brown

SNOOPY

Woodstock

Peppermint Patty

Lucy Van Pelt

Marcie

Sally Brown

LinusVan Pelt

Rerun Van Pelt

Franklin

Schroeder

Pigpen

はしがき

　本テキストは，英語にあまり自信がない大学生のために，スヌーピーが登場するマンガを用いて文法・語法の基礎と日常表現を習得できるように編集されています。全部で20のユニットで構成されていて，どのユニットも同じ構成になっています。各セッションについて簡単に説明しておきます。

. . . .

■ LET'S LEARN

● WORDS TO REMEMBER

語彙を習得するための穴埋め問題です。

● EXPRESSIONS TO REMEMBER

【LET'S TRY】の[C]に出てくる英語表現です。カッコを埋めて英文を完成させてみましょう。

● GRAMMAR AND USAGE TO REMEMBER

文法・語法の解説です。しっかり自分のものにして，例文を和訳してみましょう。

■ LET'S READ

スヌーピーのマンガを和訳してみましょう。

■ LET'S TRY

[A] 2択の文法・語法選択問題です。【GRAMMAR AND USAGE TO REMEMBER】を復習します。

[B] 文法・語法穴埋め問題，または和文英訳問題です。【GRAMMAR AND USAGE TO REMEMBER】を復習します。

[C] 整序作文問題です。【LET'S READ】に出てくる表現や語句を復習します。

[D] 3択の文法・語法選択問題です。【GRAMMAR AND USAGE TO REMEMBER】を復習します。

[E] 4択の文法・語法選択問題です。【GRAMMAR AND USAGE TO REMEMBER】を復習します。

■ INDEX

予習の参考にしてください。

■ LET'S READ MORE

英文読解問題です。和訳にトライしてみましょう。

. . . .

　本テキストの編集にあたり，各種辞書類，参考書，文法書など数多くの文献を参考にさせていただきました。本テキストはこれらの文献に負うところが多いことを記して謝辞といたします。

　最後に，本テキストの編集・出版にあたり，いろいろお世話になった朝日出版社の朝日英一郎氏と関麻央里氏，読解問題を作成し，すべての英文をていねいにチェックしていただいたスノードン英美理京子氏に，心から感謝を申し上げます。

2019年　初夏　　**編著者**

CONTENTS

音声再生アプリ「リスニング・トレーナー」を使った 音声ダウンロード

朝日出版社開発のアプリ、「リスニング・トレーナー（リストレ）」を使えば、教科書の音声を スマホ、タブレットに簡単にダウンロードできます。どうぞご活用ください。

◉ アプリ【リスニング・トレーナー】の使い方

《アプリのダウンロード》

App Store または Google Play から 「リスニング・トレーナー」のアプリ （無料）をダウンロード

App Storeは こちら▶

Google Playは こちら▶

《アプリの使い方》

① アプリを開き「コンテンツを追加」をタップ
② 画面上部に【15650】を入力しDoneをタップ

音声ストリーミング配信 》》》

この教科書の音声は、 右記ウェブサイトにて 無料で配信しています。

https://text.asahipress.com/free/english/

Happy Days with SNOOPY

- A Basic English Handbook -

品詞
PARTS OF SPEECH

WORDS TO REMEMBER 語群・頭文字をヒントにカッコを埋めてみよう。

(1) おしゃべりする　（　　　　　　　　　　　）

(2) かご　（　　　　　　　　　）

(3) 刺激的な　（　　　　　　　　　）

(4) 施設　（　　　　　　　　）

(5) 明白な　（　　　　　　　　）

(6) 〜を保証する　（　　　　　　　　　）

(7) 古代の　（ a 　　　　　　　）

(8) 独立　（ i 　　　　　　　）

(9) 毎日　（ d 　　　　　　）

(10) 夕立　（ s 　　　　　　）

［語群］

《 chat ／ evident ／ facilities ／ guarantee ／ hamper ／ stimulating 》

EXPRESSIONS TO REMEMBER カッコを埋めて英文を完成させてみよう。

1 equip A with B ／ AにBを装備する

どの車もシートベルトを装備しなければならない。

Every car must (　　　　) (　　　　) (　　　　) (　　　　)
(　　　　).

2 move to A ／ Aに引っ越す

ブラウンさん一家は先月ボストンに引っ越した。

The Browns (　　　　) (　　　　) (　　　　) (　　　　) (　　　　).

3 retire from A ／ Aを退職する

彼女は65歳で会社を退職した。

She (　　　) (　　　) (　　　) (　　　) at the age of 65 .

4 tell A of B ／ AにBについて話す

リサは私にパーティーのことを話してくれた。

Lisa (　　　) (　　　) (　　　) (　　　) (　　　).

 GRAMMAR AND USAGE TO REMEMBER 例文を和訳してみよう。

1 名詞・代名詞・冠詞

🐾 oceanのような「名詞」は名前を表すことば，youのような「代名詞」は名詞の代わりをすることば，aやtheのような「冠詞」は名詞の前に置くことばである。

🐾 冠詞と前置詞の間には名詞がくる。動詞の目的語には名詞がくる。-tion, -cy，-ance は名詞語尾。

例1 ▶ *They* speak French in Tahiti. ［代名詞］

_____

2 動詞・助動詞

🐾 wonderのような「動詞」は状態や動作を表すことば，canのような「助動詞」は動詞を助けることばである。

🐾 動詞になるものは，時制をもっているもの，〈助動詞＋動詞の原形〉，〈be動詞＋現在分詞［過去分詞］〉，〈have＋過去分詞〉であり，動詞にならないものは，〈to＋動詞の原形〉，単独の現在分詞［過去分詞］である。

例2 ▶ You *must not chat* during class. ［〈助動詞＋動詞の原形〉］

_____

3 形容詞・副詞

🐾 small, historic（歴史的に重要な）のような「形容詞」は名詞を説明することば，often, regularly（定期的に）のような「副詞」は動詞・形容詞・ほかの副詞を修飾することばである。

例3 ▶ The government is *slow* to recognize a change in the economic situation.　［形容詞］

_____

例4 ▶ The country's economy is improving *slowly* but *surely*.　［副詞］

_____

- 🐾 所有格の代名詞と名詞の間には形容詞がくる。-al, -ic は形容詞語尾。
- 🐾 副詞の後ろには形容詞がくる。-able は形容詞語尾。
- 🐾 be動詞と過去分詞 (*done*) の間には副詞がくる。-ly は副詞語尾。

4 **前置詞・接続詞**

- 🐾 from, for (〜の間) のような「前置詞」は名詞・代名詞の前に置くことば, if のような「接続詞」は語句と語句や文と文などをつなぐことばである。

例5 ▶ We heard some unusual noises soon *after takeoff*.　［〈前置詞+名詞〉］

_____

例6 ▶ He began growing flowers *after* he moved to the suburbs.
［〈文+接続詞+文〉］

_____

- 🐾 前置詞の後ろには名詞か動名詞 (*doing*) がくる。

例7 ▶ She left *without saying* goodbye to me.　［〈前置詞+動名詞〉］

_____

5 **間投詞**

- 🐾 「間投詞」は間に入れることばで, 強い感情を表したり, 相手の注意をひいたりする。

例8 ▶ How about some wine? — *Oh*, thank you.　［間投詞］

_____

【意外に用心深いウッドストック!】

🐾 oceanは名詞、youは代名詞、wonderは動詞、canは助動詞、oftenは副詞、fromは前置詞、ifは接続詞。

* Snoopy 「スヌーピー」 スポーツ万能, 趣味は小説を書くこと。好きな食べ物はピザとアイスクリーム。飼い主Charlie Brown（チャーリー・ブラウン）をはじめとする人間をからかったりするのも好き。

* Woodstock 「ウッドストック」 まっすぐ飛ぶのが苦手な渡り鳥。スヌーピーの忠実な秘書であり, 大親友。彼の言葉はスヌーピーにしか理解できない。

① I've often wondered if you can see the ocean from there.

② No?　Then I think you can take the life jacket off.

A カッコ内の適当なものを選んでみよう。

1. インドは1947年に独立を宣言した。

   India (proclamation ∕ proclaimed) its independence in 1947.

2. 言語を理解するには，文法を学ぶことが非常に重要だ。

   Learning grammar is of great (significance ∕ significantly) to understanding a language.

3. 古代ギリシャ人たちは地球の大きさを驚くほど正確に測った。

   The ancient Greeks measured the size of the earth with surprising (accuracy ∕ accurate).

B カッコを埋めて英文を完成させてみよう。

1. 私は10年間ずっと，このクマのぬいぐるみを持っています。

   I've had this teddy bear (　　　　　　) ten years.

2. 医者は私に定期的に運動するよう指示した。

   The doctor instructed me to exercise (　　　　　　).

3. 私はスペイン旅行したとき，コルドバの歴史地区を訪れた。

   When I traveled in Spain, I visited the (　　　　　　) center of Cordoba.

C カッコ内の語句を並べかえて，英文を完成させてみよう。

1. これはお探しの本ではありませんか。(wonder if...)

   I [looking ∕ the book ∕ if ∕ is ∕ not ∕ this ∕ for ∕ wonder ∕ you're].

   _____.

2. 日本はもっと市場を解放すべきだと思う。(think that …)

I [a great extent / its / Japan / markets / open / should / that / think / to].

_____ .

3. 着ていた汚れた服を脱ぎ，洗濯かごに入れた。(take off A)

I [and / my dirty / hamper / in / them / took off / put / clothes / the laundry].

_____ .

D 下線部に入る最も適当なものを選んでみよう。

1. From the _____ of the car, it was evident that it had hardly been used.

    (A) condition   **(B)** conditional   **(C)** conditionally

2. He told his wife of his _____ decision to retire from the company next year.

    (A) final   **(B)** finalize   **(C)** finally

3. No seats for the classical concert are guaranteed unless you make _____ and payments in advance.

    (A) reservations   **(B)** reserve   **(C)** reserved

E 下線部に入る最も適当なものを選んでみよう。

1. The weather here is very _____ year-round, though there are showers almost daily from December through March.

    (A) agree   **(B)** agreeable   **(C)** agreeably   **(D)** agreement

2. Bicycles are _____ used instead of cars in the Netherlands, which is well equipped with bike lanes and other bike facilities.

    (A) frequency   **(B)** frequent   **(C)** frequently   **(D)** infrequent

3. After _____ lived in a small town in Ohio for five years, Ms. Swanson wants to move to a more stimulating city like New York.

    (A) had   **(B)** have   **(C)** having   **(D)** to have

Unit 2

動詞
VERBS

LET'S LEARN

WORDS TO REMEMBER　語群・頭文字をヒントにカッコを埋めてみよう。

（ 1 ） 海外で　（　　　　　　　　　　）

（ 2 ） 建設　（　　　　　　　　　）

（ 3 ） 頼っている　（　　　　　　　　　）

（ 4 ） 展示品　（　　　　　　　　）

（ 5 ） 夕暮れ　（　　　　　　　）

（ 6 ） 良好な　（　　　　　　　）

（ 7 ） 印象　（　i　　　　　　　）

（ 8 ） 水族館　（　a　　　　　　　）

（ 9 ） 性格　（　c　　　　　　　）

（10） 便　（　f　　　　　　　）

[語群]

《 construction ／ dependent ／ exhibit ／ favorable ／ nightfall ／ overseas 》

EXPRESSIONS TO REMEMBER　カッコを埋めて英文を完成させてみよう。

1　ahead of schedule ／ 予定より早く

プロジェクトは予定より1週間早く進んでいます。

The project is running (　　　　) (　　　　) (　　　　)

(　　　　) (　　　　).

2　*be* interested in *doing* ／ ～することに興味がある

ホームレスの支援に興味はありますか？

Would you (　　　　) (　　　　) (　　　　) (　　　　) the homeless?

3 thanks to A／Aのおかげで

奨学金のおかげで大学を出ることができた。

(　　　) (　　　　) (　　　　) (　　　　　　　), I was able to finish college.

4 would like to *do*／〜したい

朝食には何を召し上がりたいですか？

(　　　) (　　　　) (　　　　) (　　　　) (　　　　) (　　　　)
for breakfast?

GRAMMAR AND USAGE TO REMEMBER　例文を和訳してみよう。

1 自動詞・他動詞

> 語の動作・状態を表す動詞を形態上で分類すると、「〜を」「〜が」「〜に」などが表す目的語を必要としない「自動詞」と、目的語を必要とする「他動詞」に分けることができる。

例1 ▶ I *ran* to the station as fast as I could. ［自動詞］

_____

例2 ▶ She *runs* a beauty parlor in Los Angeles. ［他動詞］

_____

2 5文型

> 5文型では、第1文型 (S [主語] +V [動詞]) と第2文型 (S+V+C [補語]) の動詞が自動詞で、第3文型 (S+V+O [目的語])、第4文型 (S+V+O+O)、第5文型 (S+V+O+C) の動詞が他動詞である。

例3 ▶ There *was a big fire* near my house last night. ［第1文型］

_____

例4 ▶ Canberra *is the capital* of Australia. ［第2文型］

_____

Unit 2

例5 ▶　Do you *know how to cook* this fish?　［第3文型］

_____

例6 ▶　He *gives us the impression* that he's still dependent on his parents.　［第4文型］

_____

例7 ▶　She *makes it a rule* to take a shower in the morning.　［第5文型］

_____

3　他動詞と誤りやすい自動詞

🐾　他動詞と誤りやすい自動詞には，apologize to～（～［人］に謝る），apologize for～（～［行為］を謝る），arrive at [in]～（～に到着する），belong to～（～に所属する），graduate from～（～を卒業する），listen to～（～を聞く），object to～（～に反対する），reply to～（～に答える）などがある。

例8 ▶　He *graduated from* Brown University in 2017.　［他動詞と誤りやすい自動詞］

_____

例9 ▶　You shouldn't open or *reply to* email messages from unknown senders.　［他動詞と誤りやすい自動詞］

_____

4　自動詞と誤りやすい他動詞

🐾　自動詞と誤りやすい他動詞には，approach～（～に近づく），attend～（～に出席する），discuss～（～について議論する），enter～（～に入る），include～（～を含む），marry～（～と結婚する），reach～（～に到着する），resemble～（～に似ている）などがある。

例10 ▶　A big typhoon is *approaching* Okinawa.　［自動詞と誤りやすい他動詞］

_____

例11 ▶　I *resemble* my sister in looks but not in character.
　　　　［自動詞と誤りやすい他動詞］

_____

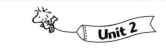

LET'S READ

マンガを和訳してみよう

【主人が心病んでいるから…】

🐾 goは目的語を必要としない自動詞，buyは目的語を必要とする他動詞。

＊ Charlie Brown「チャーリー・ブラウン」スヌーピーの飼い主。やることなすことすべてが裏目に出てヘマばかりだが，愛すべき存在。

＊ Here we go!「はい，どうぞ」

＊ (has) gone by「過ぎてしまった」

① Here we go!　It's suppertime!

_____

② Can you believe it?　Another day gone by, and it's suppertime again!

_____

③ I don't know where the time goes.　You get up in the morning, and you go to bed at night, and another day is gone.

_____

④ Someday I'm going to have to buy my own can opener.

_____

011

A カッコ内の適当なものを選んでみよう。

1. 彼の祖父は団塊世代に属する。

   His grandfather (belongs / belongs to) the baby boomer generation.

2. 彼女は知り合って3週間にしかならないのに結婚した。

   She (married / married with) someone she had only known for three weeks.

3. 電車で通勤するときにはいつもデジタル音楽プレーヤーを聞く。

   I always (listen / listen to) my digital music player while commuting by train.

B 日本文を英語に直してみよう。

1. 多くの英単語が日本語に入っている。

   _____.

2. 私たちは6月8日の夕方に成田に着いた。

   _____.

3. 学生たちは夏休みの計画 (their plans for ～) について話し合った。

   _____.

C カッコ内の語句を並べかえて，英文を完成させてみよう。

1. もう寝る時間ですよ。(go to bed)

   I [bed / for / go / it's / think / time / to / to / you].

   _____.

2. 若いころ毎朝6時に起きたものです。(get up)

   I [at / every / got / I / morning / six / up / was / when / young].

   _____.

3. ニュージーランドに行きたければ貯金しなければならないだろう。(have to *do*)

You [go / have / if / New Zealand / save up / to / to / to / want / will / you].

_____

_____.

D 下線部に入る最も適当なものを選んでみよう。

1. They strongly _____ the construction of a new airport.

    (A) object   **(B)** object to   **(C)** object with

2. After a long walk, we finally _____ the village before nightfall.

    (A) arrived   **(B)** got   **(C)** reached

3. Students interested in working overseas should _____ the sessions of the seminar.

    (A) attend   **(B)** attend at   **(C)** attend to

E 下線部に入る最も適当なものを選んでみよう。

1. I would like to _____ everyone for not being able to attend the award ceremony in person.

    (A) apologize   **(B)** apologize for   **(C)** apologize to   **(D)** apologize with

2. Some of the exhibits at the aquarium _____ fish commonly found along rocky shorelines.

    (A) include   **(B)** include in   **(C)** include to   **(D)** include with

3. Thanks to favorable wind conditions, Koala Airlines Flight 990 _____ the International Airport one hour ahead of schedule.

    (A) arrived   **(B)** arrived at   **(C)** arrived for   **(D)** arrived to

Unit 3

句動詞
PHRASAL VERBS

LET'S LEARN

WORDS TO REMEMBER 語群・頭文字をヒントにカッコを埋めてみよう。

(1) 構造 　（　　　　　　　　　）

(2) 失礼な 　（　　　　　　　　　）

(3) 退屈な 　（　　　　　　　　　）

(4) 人影 　（　　　　　　　　　）

(5) 〜を断る 　（　　　　　　　　　）

(6) 〜を設置する 　（　　　　　　　　　）

(7) 委員会 　（ c 　　　　　　　）

(8) 起源 　（ o 　　　　　　　）

(9) 展示会 　（ e 　　　　　　　）

(10) 振る舞い 　（ b 　　　　　　　）

[語群]

《 boring ／ establish ／ figure ／ refuse ／ rude ／ structure 》

EXPRESSIONS TO REMEMBER カッコを埋めて英文を完成させてみよう。

1 give up A ／ Aをあきらめる；Aを譲る

　　ケンはいつも電車でお年寄りに席を譲る。

　　Ken always (　　　　　) (　　　　　) (　　　　　) (　　　　　)

　　on the train to older people.

2 move into A／Aに引っ越す

私たちの会社はまもなく新しいビルに移転します。

Our company is (　　　　) (　　　　) (　　　　) (　　　　)

(　　　　) soon.

3 look down on A／Aを軽蔑する

理由はどうであれ人々を見下してはいけない。

(　　　　) (　　　　) (　　　　) (　　　　) (　　　　),

whatever the reason.

4 pretend to *do*／〜するふりをする

私は戸口のその人影に気づかないふりをした。

I (　　　　) (　　　　) (　　　　) (　　　　) the figure in

the doorway.

GRAMMAR AND USAGE TO REMEMBER　例文を和訳してみよう。

1 句動詞

🐾 getやtakeのような基本動詞に，inやupのような前置詞・副詞などがついた
語のまとまりが1つの動詞と同じ働きをするものを「句動詞」という。

2 〈動詞＋副詞〉で自動詞の働きをする句動詞

🐾 〈動詞＋副詞〉で自動詞の働きをする句動詞には，break down（故障する），
call out（叫ぶ），look out（気をつける），show up（姿を見せる）などがある。

例2 ▶　I *called out*, but there was no answer.　［〈動詞＋副詞〉］

_____

3 〈動詞＋前置詞〉で他動詞の働きをする句動詞

🐾 〈動詞＋前置詞〉で他動詞の働きをする句動詞には，bring about〜（〜をもた
らす），come across〜（〜に偶然出会う），consist in〜（〜にある），consist
of〜（〜から成る），deal with〜（〜を扱う），look for〜（〜をさがす），
look into〜（〜を調査する）などがある。

例2 ▶ I *came across* an interesting book in a bookstore yesterday.

［〈動詞＋前置詞＋目的語〉］

④ 〈動詞＋副詞〉で他動詞の働きをする句動詞

🐾 〈動詞＋副詞〉で他動詞の働きをする句動詞には，bring up〜（〜を育てる），carry out〜（〜を実行する），give up〜（〜をやめる；〜をあきらめる），hand in〜（〜を提出する），look over〜（〜を点検する），make out〜（〜を理解する），put off〜（〜を延期する），see off〜（〜を見送る）などがある。

例3 ▶ The tax agent *looked over* my tax form very carefully.

［〈動詞＋副詞＋目的語〉］

🐾 目的語が名詞の場合には〈動詞＋副詞＋名詞〉と〈動詞＋名詞＋副詞〉の両方が可能だが，目的語が代名詞の場合には〈動詞＋代名詞＋副詞〉の語順になる。

例4 ▶ The handwriting in this letter is so poor I can't *make it out*.

［〈動詞＋代名詞＋副詞〉］

⑤ 〈動詞＋副詞［名詞］＋前置詞〉で他動詞の働きをする句動詞

🐾 〈動詞＋副詞［名詞］＋前置詞〉で他動詞の働きをする句動詞には，go up to〜（〜のところへ行く），look down on〜（〜を軽蔑する），look up to〜（〜を尊敬する），put up with〜（〜に耐える），find fault with〜（〜のあらさがしをする），make use of〜（〜を活用する），take advantage of〜（〜を利用する）などがある。

例5 ▶ I can no longer *put up with* her rude behavior.

［〈動詞＋副詞＋前置詞＋目的語〉］

例6 ▶ He *took advantage of* the good weather to do the laundry.

［〈動詞＋名詞＋前置詞＋目的語〉］

【ウサちゃんのが欲しかったのに！】

🐾　look for～（～をさがす）は〈動詞＋前置詞〉で他動詞の働きをする句動詞。

＊bunny「ウサちゃん」

＊plain「何も描いていない」

① Yes, ma'am.　We're looking for a new supper dish.

_____

② Do you have any with pictures of bunnies on the side?　He likes bunnies.

_____

③ All right, we'll just take a plain one then.

_____

④ My life is so boring.

_____

LET'S TRY

A カッコ内の適当なものを選んでみよう。

1. インターネットは私たちの生活に変化をもたらした。

   The Internet has brought (about / down) changes in our lives.

2. この村の魅力は美しい風景にある。

   The charm of this village consists (in / of) its beautiful scenery.

3. 私はいつも子どもたちを見送りにスクールバスの停留所まで行く。

   I always go to the school bus stop to see the children (off / through).

B カッコを埋めて英文を完成させてみよう。

1. うちのエアコンは夏の一番暑い日に故障してしまった。

   Our air conditioner (　　　　　) down on the hottest day of summer.

2. その子どもたちは生まれたのは日本だが, アメリカ人として育てられた。

   Though born in Japan, the children were (　　　　　) up as Americans.

3. 英語を学ぶうえでは辞書を十分に活用することが大切だ。

   (　　　　　) good use of your dictionary is important when studying English.

C カッコ内の語句を並べかえて, 英文を完成させてみよう。

1. 家にひとりぼっちでいるのは死ぬほど退屈だ。(形容詞 boring)

   It's [all by / at / deadly boring / home / myself / stay / to].

   _____.

2. 父はいつも老眼鏡をさがしています。(look for A)

   My father [always / for / glasses / his / is / looking / reading].

   _____.

3. ポケットに手を入れたままで先生に話しかけてはいけない。(with A C)

Don't [your hands / your pockets / in / speak / the teacher / to / with].

_____.

D 下線部に入る最も適当なものを選んでみよう。

1. Jack _____ up to the post office window and bought some stamps.

    (A) put   **(B)** took   **(C)** went

2. Geology deals _____ the origin, history, and structure of the earth.

    (A) in   **(B)** up   **(C)** with

3. When I lost my job, we had to give _____ our house and move into an apartment.

    (A) through   **(B)** to   **(C)** up

E 下線部に入る最も適当なものを選んでみよう。

1. The government established a committee to look _____ the problem of unemployment.

    (A) for   **(B)** from   **(C)** in   **(D)** into

2. Lucy pretends to _____ down on football, but she never refuses a date with a football player.

    (A) get   **(B)** look   **(C)** make   **(D)** take

3. If the weather had not been so bad, more visitors would have shown _____ for the exhibition.

    (A) at   **(B)** in   **(C)** to   **(D)** up

Unit 4

基本時制
TENSES

WORDS TO REMEMBER 語群・頭文字をヒントにカッコを埋めてみよう。

（ 1 ） 揮発性の　（　　　　　　　　　　）

（ 2 ） 植物の　（　　　　　　　　）

（ 3 ） 部分　（　　　　　　　　）

（ 4 ） 方法論　（　　　　　　　　）

（ 5 ） 矛盾する　（　　　　　　　　）

（ 6 ） 読み書きのできない　（　　　　　　　　　）

（ 7 ） 基金　（ f　　　　　　　）

（ 8 ） 地元の　（ l　　　　　　　　）

（ 9 ） 難民　（ r　　　　　　　　）

（10） 利用できる；入手できる　（ a　　　　　　　　　）

［語群］

《 botanical ／ conflicting ／ illiterate ／ methodology ／ portion ／ volatile 》

EXPRESSIONS TO REMEMBER カッコを埋めて英文を完成させてみよう。

1 donate A to B ／ A を B に寄付する

その難民基金にお金を寄付した。

I (　　　　) (　　　　) (　　　　) the refugee fund.

2 go on a trip ／ 旅行に出かける

うちの両親は西海岸への旅に出かけます。

My parents are (　　　　) (　　　　) (　　　　) (　　　　)

(　　　　) the west coast.

3 as long as... ／ …さえすれば

冷たければどんな飲み物でもいいよ。

Any kind of drink will do (　　　　) (　　　　) (　　　　)

(　　　　) (　　　　) (　　　　).

4 as soon as... ／ …するとすぐに

テーブルが空き次第お名前をお呼びします。

I'll call you (　　　　) (　　　　) (　　　　) (　　　　)

(　　　　) is available.

 GRAMMAR AND USAGE TO REMEMBER 例文を和訳してみよう。

1 現在時制

🐾 「基本時制」には，「現在時制」「過去時制」「未来時制」がある。

🐾 現在時制の用法には，現在の状態を表す用法，現在の習慣 (いつもすること) を表す用法，長期にわたる事実や，過去・現在・未来にわたる一般的真理を表す用法，確定的な予定・計画を表す用法 [未来を表す副詞 (句) を伴うことが多い]，「時」(when, after, until, as soon as などに導かれる) や「条件」(if, unless, as long as などに導かれる) を表す副詞節で未来のことを表す用法がある。

例1 ▶ I usually *eat* toast for breakfast. ［現在時制／現在の習慣］

_____

例2 ▶ Three times thirteen *equals* thirty-nine. ［現在時制／一般的真理］

_____

🐾 現在時制は，each month (毎月)，every two years (2 年ごとに) といった「現在」を表す語句をよく伴う。

2 過去時制

🐾 過去時制の用法には，過去の動作・事実を表す用法，過去の状態を表す用法，過去の習慣を表す用法，現在完了の代用，時制の一致，過去完了の代用 (大過去)，不変の真理を表す用法がある。

例3 ▶ The bus *started* before I reached the bus stop. ［過去時制／過去完了の代用］

_____

🐾 過去時制は, last Friday (先週の金曜日), in 1990 (1990年に), last summer (昨年の夏) といった「過去」を表す語句をよく伴う。

③ 未来時制

🐾 未来時制〈will [shall] ＋動詞の原形〉には,「単純未来」と「意志未来」がある。単純未来は, 自分の意志ではコントロールできない動作や状態を表し, 意志未来は「〜するつもりだ」のように, 自分の意志でコントロールできる動作を表す。

例4 ▶ I *will be* twenty next year. ［単純未来］

_____

例5 ▶ I *will never forget* your kindness. ［意志未来］

_____

🐾 相手の意志を尋ねたり,「依頼」「勧誘」などの相手の気持ちを尋ねる場合には, ふつうwillを用いるが,「申し出」「提案」にはshallを用いる。

例6 ▶ *Shall* I help you with the dishes? ［「申し出」を表すshall］

_____

例7 ▶ *Shall* we go for a walk? ［「提案」を表すshall］

_____

🐾 未来時制は, next spring (来春), tomorrow (明日), next week (来週) といった「未来」を表す語句をよく伴う。

【ブツブツ言ってないで早く食事にしよう!】

🐾 主節の動詞が過去形 (thought) の場合は，現在形の助動詞は時制の一致を受けて過去形の助動詞 might に変化する。

＊Sally「サリー」チャーリー・ブラウンの妹。性格は気が強く，物事を何でも簡単に解決しようとする。学校の勉強が大嫌い。

① What's he doing in here?　It's raining so I thought he might prefer to eat indoors.

_____

② I'm supposed to eat at the same table with a dog?

_____

③ This is my bread plate.　Your bread plate is the one on the left.

_____

LET'S TRY

A カッコ内の適当なものを選んでみよう。

1. 月は地球のまわりを回っている。

   The moon (goes ／ will go) around the earth.

2. 空港に着いたらあなたに電話します。

   I'll call you when I (get ／ will get) to the airport.

3. 昨年の夏はよく海に泳ぎに行ったものです。

   I often (go ／ went) swimming in the sea last summer.

B カッコを埋めて英文を完成させてみよう。

1. 湾岸戦争は1990年にあった。

   The Gulf War (　　　　　) (　　　　　) in 1990.

2. 来週, 私はスマートフォンを買うつもりだ。

   I (　　　　　) (　　　　　) a smartphone next week.

3. 申し訳ありませんが, 母は明日, 家におりません。

   I'm sorry, but my mother (　　　　　) (　　　　　) home tomorrow.

C カッコ内の語句を並べかえて, 英文を完成させてみよう。

1. ビンセントは私にあとでもう一度電話すると言った。（時制の一致）

   Vincent [again later ／ call ／ he ／ me ／ me ／ that ／ told ／ would].

   _____.

2. 私は田舎より大都会に住むほうがいい。（prefer to *do*）

   I [a big ／ in ／ in ／ city ／ live ／ prefer ／ rather than ／ the country ／ to].

   _____.

3. 家に入るときには靴を脱ぐことになっています。(*be* supposed to *do*)

You [a home / are / enter / shoes off / supposed / take / to / when / you / your].

_____

_____ .

D 下線部に入る最も適当なものを選んでみよう。

1. The students _____ on a field trip to the botanical gardens last Friday.

     (A) go   (B) went   (C) will go

2. Mr. Chen _____ a course on digital marketing at a local university next spring.

     (A) takes   (B) took   (C) will take

3. Flight arrivals _____ on the monitors as soon as the information becomes available.

     (A) posted   (B) were posted   (C) will be posted

E 下線部に入る最も適当なものを選んでみよう。

1. As long as the volatile matter _____ stored properly in a cool place, it will not be dangerous.

     (A) be   (B) is   (C) was   (D) will be

2. Each month, the museum _____ a portion of the proceeds from their exhibit to the Marlow Library for the illiterate.

     (A) donate   (B) donated   (C) donates   (D) will donate

3. Although the two studies used similar methodologies and were conducted at roughly the same time, they _____ some conflicting research results.

     (A) have yield   (B) will yield   (C) yield   (D) yielded

Unit 5

進行形・完了形
PROGRESSIVE FORM AND PERFECT TENSE

LET'S LEARN

WORDS TO REMEMBER　語群・頭文字をヒントにカッコを埋めてみよう。

（1）裏の　（　　　　　　　　　　　　）

（2）許可　（　　　　　　　　　　　　）

（3）心優しい　（　　　　　　　　　　　　）

（4）巡回の　（　　　　　　　　　　）

（5）〜を得る　（　　　　　　　　　　）

（6）〜を開催する　（　　　　　　　　　　　）

（7）甥　（ n　　　　　　　　　）

（8）高速道路　（ e　　　　　　　　　　　）

（9）花　（ b　　　　　　　　　）

（10）〜を修理する　（ f　　　　　　　　　　　）

［語群］

《 approval ／ heartwarming ／ host ／ obtain ／ rear ／ traveling 》

EXPRESSIONS TO REMEMBER　カッコを埋めて英文を完成させてみよう。

1　at the beginning of A ／ A の初めに

彼女は4月の初めにカナダに向かった。

She left for Canada (　　　　　) (　　　　　) (　　　　　)

(　　　　　) (　　　　　).

2 by the time… ／ …するときまでには

あなたが家に着くころまでには夕食の準備ができています。

Dinner will be ready (　　　) (　　　) (　　　)
(　　　) (　　　) (　　　).

3 finish *doing* ／ ～し終える

その本を読み終えたら私に貸してくれませんか？

Will you lend me the book after you've (　　　) (　　　)
(　　　)?

4 help A *do* ／ Aが～するのを手伝う

彼は甥がその会社に就職できるように手助けをした。

He (　　　) (　　　) (　　　) (　　　) (　　　)
(　　　) in the company.

GRAMMAR AND USAGE TO REMEMBER　例文を和訳してみよう。

1 現在進行形・過去進行形・未来進行形

🐾 「現在進行形」は〈is [are／am]＋現在分詞（動詞の原形＋-ing）〉という形で,「今
～している」という意味を表し, 現在進行中の動作や動作の継続状態, 確定
的な未来, 行為の反復, 行為者の習慣などを表す。

例1 ▶ The river *is flowing* very fast after last night's rain. ［現在進行形］

_____

🐾 「過去進行形」は〈was [were]＋現在分詞〉という形で,「そのとき～していた」
という意味を表し, 過去のある時点での進行中・継続中の動作, 過去の時点
での近い未来, 過去における行為の反復を表す。

例2 ▶ Ted *was washing* his car when I called on him. ［過去進行形］

_____

🐾 「未来進行形」は〈will be＋現在分詞〉という形で,「未来のあるとき～してい
るだろう」という意味を表し, 未来のある時点での進行中・継続中の動作,
現時点での近い未来の予定, 未来における行為の反復を表す。

例3 ▶ She *will be flying* over the Pacific about this time tomorrow.
［未来進行形］

---

2 進行形にできない動詞

🐾 「知覚・感覚」を表す動詞 (feel「感じる」, taste「味がする」)，「状態」を表す動詞 (be「〜である」, belong「属する」, resemble「似ている」)，「心理状態」を表す動詞 (believe「信じる」, think「思う」, like「好む」) などは進行形にできない。

例4 ▶ I *belong* to the drama club. ［進行形にできない動詞］

例5 ▶ Which season do you *like* best? ［進行形にできない動詞］

---

3 現在完了形・過去完了形・未来完了形

🐾 「現在完了形」は〈have [has] ＋過去分詞〉の形で，現在を基準にして，現在までの完了・結果・経験・継続を表す。現在完了形は，現在に意識が向き，現在の状態がどうであるかを述べるため，明らかに過去を表す語句や明らかに答えに過去の時を求めている疑問詞whenとともに用いることはできない。

例6 ▶ There *has been* no rain here for the past three weeks. ［現在完了形］

🐾 「過去完了形」は〈had ＋過去分詞〉の形で，過去を基準として，過去までの完了・結果・経験・継続を表す。また，過去よりさらに過去であること (大過去) を示す場合にも用いられる。

例7 ▶ I *had* not *read* a few pages before I fell asleep. ［過去進行形］

🐾 「未来完了形」は〈will have ＋過去分詞〉の形で，未来のある時を基準にして，その時までの完了・結果・経験・状態の継続を表す。また，「時」や「条件」を表す副詞節では未来完了形の代わりに現在完了形を用いる。

例8 ▶ If I read this book again, I'*ll have read* it ten times. ［未来完了形］

【プレッシャーがかかって…】

🐾　am having は「今〜している」という意味を表す現在進行形。

＊Lucy 「ルーシー」 おしゃべりで人を批判するのが得意。世界は自分を中心に回っている超利己主義者。

＊page turner 「ページをどんどんめくりたくなるような面白い本」

＊sweep A off A's feet 「Aを夢中にさせる」

① You should write a "page turner."

_____

② Write a book that will "sweep booksellers off their feet."

_____

③ You should write a book that is "powerful, yet heartwarming!"

_____

④ I'm having trouble with the first sentence.

_____

A カッコ内の適当なものを選んでみよう。

1. 今, 何しているの?

   What (are you doing ／ do you do) now?

2. いつその知らせを聞いたのですか?

   When (did you hear ／ have you heard) the news?

3. 現代美術はあまり好きではない。

   I (am not liking ／ don't like) modern art very much.

B カッコを埋めて英文を完成させてみよう。

1. 来月で, 私たちはここに20年間住んだことになります。

   We (   ) (   ) (   ) here for twenty years next month.

2. 先週, 野球をしているとき, 左脚を骨折した。

   I broke my left leg while I (   ) (   ) baseball last week.

3. 来年の今ごろはカナダのある大学で勉強していることだろう。

   This time next year I (   ) (   ) (   ) at some university in Canada.

C カッコ内の語句を並べかえて, 英文を完成させてみよう。

1. 宿題で何か困ったことはありませんか? （have trouble with A）

   Do [any ／ have ／ homework ／ trouble ／ with ／ you ／ your]?

   _____ ?

2. 外国語を少なくとも1つは習得したほうがいいよ。(You should *do*)

You [at / foreign / least / master / one / language / should].

_____.

3. アメリカ史に関する本はありますか？（関係代名詞 that）

Do [American / any / books / deal / have / history / that / with/ you]?

_____?

D 下線部に入る最も適当なものを選んでみよう。

1. About this time next year I _____ skiing in Austria.

   (A) am　　**(B)** was　　**(C)** will be

2. Our village _____ very quiet until the expressway was built.

   (A) had been　　**(B)** has been　　**(C)** will have been

3. You should use the elevators at the rear entrance while the ones in the lobby _____ .

   (A) are being fixed　　**(B)** had been fixed　　**(C)** were being fixed

E 下線部に入る最も適当なものを選んでみよう。

1. The library _____ a traveling exhibit of miniature books at the beginning of next month.

   (A) had hosted　　**(B)** has hosted　　**(C)** is hosting　　**(D)** was hosting

2. Green Air _____ approval to perform daily flights between St. Petersburg and Brussels starting in April.

   (A) has received　　**(B)** receive　　**(C)** was receiving　　**(D)** will be receiving

3. By the time you finish reading these books, you _____ a lot of ideas and information that will help you start a successful business.

   (A) had obtained　　**(B)** has obtained　　**(C)** have obtained　　**(D)** will have obtained

Unit 6

名詞・冠詞
NOUNS AND ARTICLES

LET'S LEARN

WORDS TO REMEMBER 語群・頭文字をヒントにカッコを埋めてみよう。

（1）資源　（　　　　　　　　　　　）

（2）所有地　（　　　　　　　　　　　）

（3）地方　（　　　　　　　　　　）

（4）忠実な　（　　　　　　　　　　）

（5）満足　（　　　　　　　　　）

（6）予測のつかない　（　　　　　　　　　　　）

（7）消費者　（ c　　　　　　　　　）

（8）10年間　（ d　　　　　　　　　）

（9）正確な　（ a　　　　　　　　　）

（10）反応　（ r　　　　　　　　　）

［語群］

《 contentment ／ faithful ／ property ／ region ／ resources ／ unpredictable 》

EXPRESSIONS TO REMEMBER カッコを埋めて英文を完成させてみよう。

1 change A into B ／ AをBに変える

マジシャンはその紙をお金に変えた。

The magician (　　　　) (　　　　) (　　　　) (　　　　)
(　　　　).

2 plan to *do* ／ ～する予定である

明日そこへ行く予定です。

I'm (　　　　) (　　　　) (　　　　) (　　　　) (　　　　).

3 provide A with B ／ AにBを提供する

消費者には正確な情報を提供することが重要だ。

It is important to (　　　) (　　　) (　　　) accurate information.

4 say that... ／ …と書いてある

イタリアで洪水があったと新聞に出ている。

The paper (　　　) (　　　) (　　　) (　　　) (　　　) (　　　) in Italy.

 ## GRAMMAR AND USAGE TO REMEMBER 例文を和訳してみよう。

1 数えられる名詞・数えられない名詞

🐾 「名詞」には「数えられる名詞」と「数えられない名詞」がある。数えられる名詞は，単数形と複数形があり，単数にはaかanがつけられ，数詞がつけられたり，複数形にはmanyやfewなどの不定の数を表す語がつけられる。

例1 ▶ *Dogs* are faithful animals. ［数えられる名詞］

_____

🐾 数えられない名詞は，原則として複数形にできず，aやanの次には置けない。数詞を直接つけることはできないが，a small amount of〜（少量の〜）のような量の多少を表す語はつけることができる。

例2 ▶ *Happiness* consists in contentment. ［数えられない名詞］

_____

2 不定冠詞a／an

🐾 「冠詞」には，「不定冠詞」（a［母音で始まる語の前ではan]）と「定冠詞」（the）がある。

🐾 不定冠詞はone（1つ）からできた語で，不定のものを指し，原則として数えられる名詞の単数形につき，「ある（=certain）」「いくらかの（=some）」「〜につき（=per〜）」といった意味を表すことができる。

例3 ▶ There was not *a* cloud in the sky. ［不定冠詞／「1つの」］

_____

③ 定冠詞 the

🐾 定冠詞は，特定なものを指し，数えられる名詞にも，数えられない名詞にもつき，何を指すか明らかな場合，世界に１つしか存在しないと考えられる場合，単位を表す場合（〈by the＋単位の名詞〉），動作の対象となる人や動物の身体の一部を指す場合（〈by [on, in など] the＋身体の部分の名詞〉），形容詞の最上級や句・節によって限定されている場合などに用いられる。

例4 ▶ Autumn is *the* best season for reading. ［定冠詞／最上級］

_____

④ 無冠詞

🐾 呼びかけ，家族関係，官職などが補語にある場合，季節・食事・スポーツ・ゲーム名，交通・通信を表す場合（by bus「バスで」，by email「メールで」），抽象的な目的や機能など表す場合（watch TV「テレビを見る」），２つの名詞が対句になっている場合（from head to toe「全身；完全に」），慣用表現（take place「行われる」）などは「無冠詞」になる。

例5 ▶ She was elected *captain* of the school basketball team.
［無冠詞／官職などが補語にある場合］

_____

例6 ▶ I prefer talking *face to face* to talking on the phone.
［無冠詞／2つの名詞が対句になっている場合］

_____

【やられたらやりかえす！】

🐾 on the head は〈on the ＋身体の部分の名詞〉で，動作の対象となる人や動物の身体の一部を指す用法。

＊Rerun「リラン」ルーシーとライナスの弟。スヌーピーをよく遊びに誘う。

＊BONK!「ボコン!」

① BONK!

_____

② I hit you on the head so I think that means you get a free shot.

_____

③ BONK!

_____

LET'S TRY

A カッコ内の適当なものを選んでみよう。

1. 私たちは湖のまわりを1時間歩いた。

   We walked around the lake for (a / an) hour.

2. アメリカでは子どもたちはたいてい月を銀色に描きます。

   In America, kids usually draw (moon / the moon) silver.

3. 開会式は屋外で行われる予定です。

   The opening ceremony will take (a place / place) outdoors.

B 下線部を埋めて英文を完成させてみよう。

1. 私はふだんバスで通学しています。

   I usually come to school _____.

2. 1日に3回この薬を飲みなさい。

   You should take this medicine _____.

3. アルバイトの人たちは時間単位で給料が支払われる。

   People working part-time are paid _____.

C カッコ内の語句を並べかえて，英文を完成させてみよう。

1. 雨が激しく降り出したのでピクニックを中止にした。（接続詞 so ...）

   It [called / began / hard, / off / rain / so / the picnic / to / very / we].

   _____.

2. ゴールに着いたとき，コーチは私の背中をポンとたたいた。（定冠詞 the）

   When [me / I / on / patted / reached / the back / the coach / the goal,].

   _____.

3. 答案用紙の×印はあなたの答えが間違っていることを示す。（mean that...）

The crosses on [answers ／ are ／ mean ／ incorrect ／ that ／ the exam paper ／ your].

_____

_____ .

D 下線部に入る最も適当なものを選んでみよう。

1. The princess's kiss changed the ugly frog into _____.

    (A) a handsome prince   **(B)** an handsome prince

    (C) the handsome prince

2. The guidebook says that Oahu is _____ visited island in Hawaii.

    (A) a most   **(B)** most   **(C)** the most

3. _____ in this region is definitely unpredictable at this time of the year.

    (A) A weather   **(B)** The weather   **(C)** Weather

E 下線部に入る最も適当なものを選んでみよう。

1. He has been working here for almost a decade, but he is planning to move to Boston in _____ .

    (A) a spring   **(B)** spring   **(C)** springs   **(D)** the spring

2. _____ has provided us with everything we need—air, water, food, and natural resources like oil.

    (A) A nature   **(B)** An nature   **(C)** Nature   **(D)** The nature

3. If the product comes into sudden contact with even _____ water, it can cause a chemical reaction.

    (A) a large number of   **(B)** a small amount of   **(C)** few   **(D)** many

Unit 7

代名詞
PRONOUNS

LET'S LEARN

WORDS TO REMEMBER 語群・頭文字をヒントにカッコを埋めてみよう。

（1） アプリ　（　　　　　　　　　　）

（2） 深刻な　（　　　　　　　　　　）

（3） 添付の　（　　　　　　　　　　）

（4） 品質　（　　　　　　　　　　　）

（5） ～を購入する　（　　　　　　　　　　）

（6） ～を評価する　（　　　　　　　　　　）

（7） アンケート　（ q　　　　　　　　　）

（8） 家具　（ f　　　　　　　　）

（9） 環境　（ e　　　　　　　　　）

（10） ～を無視する　（ i　　　　　　　　　）

［語群］

《 app ／ attached ／ gauge ／ purchase ／ quality ／ serious 》

EXPRESSIONS TO REMEMBER カッコを埋めて英文を完成させてみよう。

1 *be* superior to A ／ Aより優れている

フランスワインが必ずしもカリフォルニアワインより上等とは限らない。

French wine is (　　　　) (　　　　) (　　　　) (　　　　)

California wine.

2 fill out A ／ Aに必要事項を記入する

この申込用紙に必要事項を記入してください。

Please (　　　　) (　　　　) (　　　　) (　　　　) (　　　　).

3 so that A can *do* ／ Aが～できるように

彼は家族に安楽な生活をさせるため一生懸命働いた。

He worked hard (　　　) (　　　　　) his family (　　　　)
(　　　　　) comfortably.

4 too C for A to *do* ／ Aが～するにはCすぎる

状況は私たちとしては無視できないほど深刻である。

The situation is (　　　　) (　　　　) (　　　　) (　　　　)
(　　　) (　　　　).

 GRAMMAR AND USAGE TO REMEMBER 例文を和訳してみよう。

1 itの注意すべき用法

🐾 itの注意すべき用法には，前出の句や節を示す用法，天候・時間・距離・寒暖などを表す用法，状況を表す用法 (Take it easy.「気楽にやれよ」)，形式主語 (It is C (for A) to *do*「(Aが)～するのはCだ」)，形式目的語 (find it C to *do*「～するのはCだとわかる」)，強調構文 (It is A that [who] ～「～なのはAだ」)，特殊構文 (It takes A B to *do*「Aが～するのにB(時間)がかかる」) などがある。

例1 ▶ *It*'s a shooting star that you saw in the sky.　[強調構文]

_____

2 we・you・theyの特殊用法

🐾 weが話し手自身を含めた一般の人々を，youが聞き手を含めた一般の人々を，theyがpeopleと同様に，世間一般の人々を指す場合がある。

例2 ▶ You can do anything when you are young.
[聞き手を含めた一般の人々を指すyou]

_____

3 it・oneとthat・those

🐾 itが前に出た「そのものずばりの特定の単数名詞」(〈the＋単数名詞〉で書き換えられる) を受けるのに対して，単独で用いられるoneはその単数名詞と「同種のもの」(〈a [an]＋単数名詞〉で書き換えられる) を受ける。

例3 ▶ I gave her a necklace and she loved *it*. ［特定の単数名詞を受ける it］

🐾 名詞の反復を避けるために，前に出た単数名詞を that で，複数名詞を those で受けることがある。

例4 ▶ The population of Tokyo is larger than *that* of New York.
［単数名詞の反復を避けるための that］

---

4 -one [-body]・-thing と -self [-selves]

🐾 「人」を表す代名詞には，someone [somebody]（誰か），anyone [anybody]（誰か；誰でも），no one [nobody]（誰も～ない），everyone [everybody]（みんな）があり単数として扱われる。

🐾 「もの」を表す代名詞には，something（何か），anything（何か；何でも），nothing（何も～ない），everything（全部）があり単数として扱われる。

例5 ▶ Machines cannot do *everything* for people. ［「もの」を表す代名詞］

🐾 -self [-selves] という形の代名詞は，主語と目的語が一致している場合に他動詞や前置詞の目的語として用いられる。

例6 ▶ You must take care of *yourself* when traveling alone.
［前置詞の目的語］

マンガを和訳してみよう

【渡り鳥なのに渡るのをよく忘れるウッドストック!】

🐾 　yourselfは，主語と目的語が一致している場合に，前置詞の目的語として用いられる。

＊ take care of *oneself* 「体に気をつける」

＊ now 「これで」

① Have a nice trip.　Take care of yourself.

_____

② ……

③ That was good.　Now you can tell everyone you flew south for the winter.

_____

_____

A カッコ内の適当なものを選んでみよう。

1. 一日中浜辺で横になっているのは楽しかったですか?

   Did you find (it / that) pleasant to lie on the beach all day?

2. 財布をあちこち捜したが見つからなかった。

   I looked everywhere for my wallet, but I couldn't find (it / one).

3. 東京での生活費は日本のほかのどの都市より高い。

   The cost of living in Tokyo is higher than (that / those) of any other city in Japan.

B 代名詞でカッコを埋めて英文を完成させてみよう。

1. スージーは階段から落ちてけがをした。

   Susie hurt (　　　　　) when she fell down the stairs.

2. 熱帯の国々では, ふつう10代で結婚します。

   In tropical countries, (　　　　　) generally marry in their teens.

3. ギリシャの山々は英国の山より木が少ない。

   The mountains of Greece are less thickly wooded than (　　　　　) of Britain.

C カッコ内の語句を並べかえて, 英文を完成させてみよう。

1. 彼女はすぐ戻ってくると私に言った。(tell A that …)

   She [be / me / right back / she / that / told / would].

   _____ .

2. 私の留守中，ナンシーが犬の世話をした。(take care of A)

Nancy [away / care / I / my dog / of / took / was / while].

_____.

3. ヨーロッパを旅行中にどのような国を訪れましたか？（名詞 trip）

What [did / during / countries / Europe / to / trip / visit / you / your]?

_____?

D 下線部に入る最も適当なものを選んでみよう。

1. Please fill out the attached questionnaire and return _____ to us.

    (A) it **(B)** one **(C)** them

2. Everyone who wanted a ticket to the concert was able to get _____ .

    (A) it **(B)** one **(C)** that

3. The furniture they bought was too heavy for them to move by _____ .

    (A) them **(B)** themselves **(C)** they

E 下線部に入る最も適当なものを選んでみよう。

1. As _____ get older, it gets more difficult to adjust ourselves to a new environment.

    (A) I **(B)** they **(C)** we **(D)** you

2. The quality of the product we choose to buy proved to be far superior to _____ of any other product in its class.

    (A) it **(B)** one **(C)** that **(D)** those

3. The new home improvement app has a free demo version so that you can gauge its value for _____ before purchasing the full package.

    (A) you **(B)** your **(C)** yours **(D)** yourself

Unit 8

形容詞
ADJECTIVES

LET'S LEARN

WORDS TO REMEMBER 語群・頭文字をヒントにカッコを埋めてみよう。

（1） 息苦しい （   ）

（2） 解決法 （   ）

（3） 通知 （   ）

（4） 日常的に （   ）

（5） 不安な （   ）

（6） 幼稚園 （   ）

（7） 警戒した （ a   ）

（8） 竜巻 （ t   ）

（9） 不可能な （ i   ）

（10） 故郷 （ h   ）

[語群]

《 kindergarten ／ nervous ／ notice ／ routinely ／ solution ／ stuffy 》

EXPRESSIONS TO REMEMBER カッコを埋めて英文を完成させてみよう。

1 It is C to do ／ 〜することはCだ

その試合のチケットを手に入れるのは不可能かもしれない。

It may (   ) (   ) (   ) (   ) (   )
for the game.

2 make A C ／ AをCにする

飛行機に乗るといつも不安になる。

Flying (   ) (   ) (   ) (   ).

3 so C that... ／とてもCなので…

テキサス人はバーベキューが大好きで，日常的に朝食で食べるくらいだ。

Texans love barbecue (　　　) (　　　) that they routinely eat it for breakfast.

4 suggest *doing* ／〜することを提案する

この問題について決をとってはいかがでしょうか?

May I (　　　) (　　　) (　　　) (　　　) on this matter?

 GRAMMAR AND USAGE TO REMEMBER) 例文を和訳してみよう。

1 形容詞の限定用法

🐾 「形容詞」は，名詞の状態・性質・数量などを表す。形容詞の中には，costly（高価な），friendly（親しみやすい），weekly（週1回の）のように，副詞の語尾-lyがつくものもある。

例1 ▶ Japan must keep a *friendly* relationship with China. ［-lyのつく形容詞］

🐾 〈形容詞＋名詞〉や rooms *available*（利用できる部屋），plants native to the region（その地域に昔からある植物）のように，〈名詞・代名詞＋形容詞〉という形で，形容詞が直接，名詞・代名詞を修飾する用法を「限定用法」という。限定用法のみの形容詞には，former（前の），further（さらなる），main（主要な），mere（ほんのちょっとした），only（唯一の），outer（外の），total（総合の），wooden（木製の）などがある。

例2 ▶ The *only* solution is telling her the whole story.

［限定用法のみの形容詞「唯一の」］

2 形容詞の叙述用法

🐾 〈主語＋動詞＋形容詞（補語）〉［第2文型］や〈主語＋動詞＋目的語＋形容詞（補語）〉［第5文型］という形で，形容詞が動詞や目的語の後ろに置かれて，補語になる用法を「叙述用法」という。叙述用法のみの形容詞には，afraid（恐れて），alive（生きている），ashamed（恥じて），asleep（眠って），glad（喜んで），content（満足して），unable（できない）などがある。

例3 ▶ I feel *ashamed* of having told such a lie to him.
　　　　［叙述用法のみの形容詞「恥じて」］

---

3 限定用法と叙述用法で意味が異なる形容詞

　　🐾 限定用法と叙述用法で意味が異なる形容詞には，certain（[限]ある；いくぶ
　　　んかの／[叙]確信している），late（[限]故〜／[叙]遅れて），present（[限]
　　　現在の／[叙]出席して [*be* present at the conference（会議に出席して）]），
　　　right（[限]右の／[叙]正しい）などがある。

4 紛らわしい形容詞

　　🐾 紛らわしい形容詞には，economic（経済の）／economical（経済的な），
　　　historic（歴史上重要な）／historical（歴史上の），respectful（尊敬して）／
　　　respectable（尊敬される）／respective（それぞれの）などがある。

例4 ▶ Shanghai is China's *economic* capital.　［「経済の」］

例5 ▶ The children returned to their *respective* hometowns.
　　　　［「それぞれの」］

LET'S READ

マンガを和訳してみよう

【言い訳はばっちり！】

🐾 　luckyはここでは叙述用法の形容詞。

＊ tell A (that) ...「Aに…だと言う」

＊ My dog ate my homework.「うちの犬に宿題を食べられちゃったんです」生徒が宿題をやってこなかったときの言い訳。

① We don't have homework in kindergarten.

_____

② I know.　You're lucky.

When we do, I'll tell the teacher my dog ate my homework.

_____

_____

③ You don't have a dog.

I'll borrow a dog.

Write your homework on a doughnut, and I'll eat it.

_____

_____

_____

LET'S TRY

A カッコ内の適当なものを選んでみよう。

1. 今日は私の亡くなった夫の誕生日です。

   Today is my (late / lately) husband's birthday.

2. そのレストランには親しみやすい雰囲気があります。

   The restaurant offers a (friend / friendly) atmosphere.

3. 仕事に行くため家を出たとき，彼はまだ寝ぼけまなこだった。

   He was still half (asleep / sleeping) when he left home for work.

B 下線部を埋めて英文を完成させてみよう。

1. 私はそのホテルに電話したが，空室はなかった。

   I called the hotel, but there were no _____.

2. すべての委員はその会議に出席しなければならない。

   All committee members must _____.

3. その植物園は，その地域に昔からあるさまざまな種類の固有植物を展示しています。

   The botanical garden displays a wide variety of _____.

C カッコ内の語句を並べかえて，英文を完成させてみよう。

1. 答案用紙の上部に名前を書きなさい。（write A）

   Write [at / answer / name / of / sheet / the / the / top / your].

   _____.

2. その会社はさらに200万ドルを銀行から借りた。（borrow A）

   The company [another / borrowed / dollars / from / million / the bank / two].

   _____.

3. 宿題を全部終えたら遊びに行っていいよ。(接続詞 when ...)

You [all of ／ and ／ go out ／ have done ／ may ／ play ／ when you ／ your homework].

_____

_____.

D 下線部に入る最も適当なものを選んでみよう。

1. For me, it is more _____ to use a taxi than to own a car.

　　(A) economic　　**(B)** economical　　**(C)** economically

2. She's so sick that she's been _____ to get out of bed for a week.

　　(A) former　　**(B)** mere　　**(C)** unable

3. The botanical garden is closed to the public until _____ notice.

　　(A) content　　**(B)** further　　**(C)** glad

E 下線部に入る最も適当なものを選んでみよう。

1. The _____ fact that he hadn't forgotten her birthday made her happy.

　　(A) content　　**(B)** glad　　**(C)** mere　　**(D)** unable

2. During tornado season, it is important to stay _____ for changing weather conditions.

　　(A) alert　　**(B)** alerted　　**(C)** alerting　　**(D)** to alert

3. It was so stuffy in the room that she suggested leaving all of the windows _____ for a while.

　　(A) open　　**(B)** opening　　**(C)** openly　　**(D)** openness

Unit 9

副詞
ADVERBS

LET'S LEARN

WORDS TO REMEMBER 語群・頭文字をヒントにカッコを埋めてみよう。

（ 1 ） 局 （　　　　　　　　　　　）

（ 2 ） 深刻さ （　　　　　　　　　　）

（ 3 ） 時間に正確な （　　　　　　　　　）

（ 4 ） 変動 （　　　　　　　　　）

（ 5 ） 〜を緩和する （　　　　　　　　　）

（ 6 ） 〜を生産する （　　　　　　　　　）

（ 7 ） ガレージ （ g　　　　　　　　　）

（ 8 ） 症状 （ s　　　　　　　　）

（ 9 ） ハイキング （ h　　　　　　　　　）

（10） 休み （ b　　　　　　　　　）

［語群］

《 manufacture ／ prompt ／ reduce ／ severity ／ station ／ variation 》

EXPRESSIONS TO REMEMBER カッコを埋めて英文を完成させてみよう。

1 *be* kind enough to *do* ／ 親切にも〜する

戸を閉めてください。

Be kind (　　　　　) (　　　　　) (　　　　　) (　　　　　) (　　　　　).

2 *be* known for A ／ Aで知られている

私たちの町は桜の花で有名です。

Our town is well (　　　　　) (　　　　　) (　　　　　) cherry

blossoms.

3 provide A for B ／ AをBに供給する

彼らは難民に食料を提供している。

They (　　　) (　　　) (　　　　) the refuges.

4 see how ... ／ どのように…かを観察する

マジシャンがトランプをどうやって切るか見ていなさい。

(　　　) (　　　　) the magician shuffles (　　　)
(　　　).

GRAMMAR AND USAGE TO REMEMBER　例文を和訳してみよう。

1 副詞の表す意味

🐾 「副詞」は，動詞，形容詞，ほかの副詞，または，shortly after〜（〜の後すぐに）のように句・節，Luckily, ...（運よく，…）のように文全体を修飾する。

例1 ▶ *Unfortunately*, the baseball game was canceled yesterday.
［文を修飾する副詞］

🐾 副詞には，「場所」を表すabroad（外国へ），here（ここに），home（家に），there（そこに），「時」を表すnow（今），soon（すぐに），today（今日），「頻度」を表すalways（いつも；いつでも [you can always leave（いつやめてもいいよ）]），never（決して〜ない），seldom（めったに〜ない），usually（ふつうは），「可能性」を表すcertainly（確実に），possibly（ひょっとすると），probably（たぶん），「程度」を表すalmost（ほとんど），completely（完全に），very（とても），「様態」を表すfast（速く），quickly（すばやく），well（上手に）などがある。

例2 ▶ Wait until the paint is *completely* dry. ［「程度」を表す副詞］

🐾 「頻度」を表す副詞は，一般動詞の前，be動詞・助動詞の後ろに置かれる。

2 -lyの有無で意味が異なる副詞

🐾 -lyの有無で意味が異なる副詞には，close（近くに）／closely（綿密に），hard（熱心に）／hardly（ほとんど〜ない），high（高く）／highly（非常に），just（ちょうど）／justly（正しく），late（遅く）／lately（最近），near（近くに）／nearly（ほとんど），pretty（かなり）／prettily（きれいに）などがある。

例3 ▶　My father has been very busy *lately* and comes home *late* every night.
　　　　［「最近」／「遅く」］

_____

③　ago・before

🐾　～agoは現在を基準とする「過去時制」で，～beforeは過去のある時点を基準とする「過去完了形」で用いられる。

例4 ▶　The boy bought the mountain bike weeks *ago*.

_____

④　enough

🐾　形容詞・副詞を修飾するenoughは，修飾する語の後ろに置かれる。

例5 ▶　This novel is easy *enough* for children to read.

_____

⑤　副詞句next～・last～の前のtheの有無

🐾　現在を基準にして「次の～」はnext～，「前の～」はlast～で，theは不要だが，過去や未来のある時点を基準にして「その次の～」はthe next～［the next week（その翌週に）］，「その前の～」はthe last～で，theが必要である。

例6 ▶　*Last week* we went on a hike around Lake Tama.

_____

Unit 9

 マンガを和訳してみよう

【食いしん坊のスヌーピー！】

🐾 veryは「程度」を表す副詞で形容詞funnyを修飾し，probablyは「可能性・確信の度合い」を表す副詞で文全体を修飾し，neverは「頻度」を表す副詞で動詞licksを修飾している。

＊ wear out A「Aをすり減らす」

① The man at the store thought it was very funny that you wear out so many supper dishes.

_____

② He said his dog has had the same dish all his life.

_____

③ He probably never licks the bottom of the dish.

_____

A カッコ内の適当なものを選んでみよう。

1. 私は職場の近くに住んでいます。

   I live (close ╱ closely) to my workplace.

2. 経済はかなり回復してきたようだ。

   The economy seems to have recovered (prettily ╱ pretty) well.

3. その3か月前に転職した，と彼女は言った。

   She said that she had changed jobs three months (ago ╱ before).

B 下線部を埋めて英文を完成させてみよう。

1. スーザンは私にも理解できるくらいゆっくりと英語を話してくれた。

   Susan spoke English _____.

2. 給料が不満だというのなら，いつやめてもいいんだよ。

   _____ if you are dissatisfied with your salary.

3. 彼らは大阪に1週間滞在して，その翌週に東京に行った。

   They stayed in Osaka for a week, and then went to Tokyo _____
   _____.

C カッコ内の語句を並べかえて，英文を完成させてみよう。

1. 彼女が1週間もメールを送ってこないなんて変だ。(It's funny that…)

   It's [a week ╱ email ╱ for ╱ funny ╱ hasn't ╱ me ╱ sent ╱ she ╱ that].

   _____.

2．その選手は今季限りで引退すると言った。(say that…)

The player [at / he / of / retire / said / the end / this season / that / would].

_____.

3．私はたくさん歩くので，毎年，靴を4足履きつぶす。(wear out A)

Because [a lot, / every / four / I / I / of shoes / out / pairs / walk / wear / year].

_____.

D 下線部に入る最も適当なものを選んでみよう。

1．He was kind _____ to drive me to the subway station.

(A) enough　　(B) pretty　　(C) well

2．The afternoon session of the conference will begin _____ after the one-hour break.

(A) hardly　　(B) high　　(C) shortly

3．The medicine works _____ effectively, reducing the severity of common cold symptoms.

(A) seldom　　(B) there　　(C) very

E 下線部に入る最も適当なものを選んでみよう。

1．Tourists will visit the main factory _____ week to see how the products are manufactured.

(A) last　　(B) next　　(C) the last　　(D) the next

2．The airport shuttle was _____ prompt, showing little variation in keeping its regular schedule.

(A) home　　(B) here　　(C) soon　　(D) usually

3．The news channel provides weather information for the entire state and the station is known for its _____ accurate reports.

(A) height　　(B) heighten　　(C) high　　(D) highly

Unit 10

助動詞
AUXILIARY VERBS

LET'S LEARN

WORDS TO REMEMBER 語群・頭文字をヒントにカッコを埋めてみよう。

（1） 仮の　　（　　　　　　　　　　　　）

（2） 締切りの　（　　　　　　　　　　　　）

（3） 申込書　（　　　　　　　　　　）

（4） 有害な　（　　　　　　　　　）

（5） 〜を提出する　（　　　　　　　　　　）

（6） 〜を配布する　（　　　　　　　　　　　）

（7） くずかご　（ w　　　　　　　　　）

（8） 装置　（ d　　　　　　　　　　）

（9） パンフレット　（ b　　　　　　　　　　　）

（10） 履歴書　（ r　　　　　　　　　　）

［語群］

《 application ／ distribute ／ due ／ harmful ／ submit ／ tentative 》

EXPRESSIONS TO REMEMBER カッコを埋めて英文を完成させてみよう。

1 insert A into B ／ A を B に挿入する

彼は穴に手を突っ込んで箱をとり出した。

He (　　　　) (　　　　) (　　　　) (　　　　) the hole and
pulled out a box.

2 note that... ／ …ということに注意する

小切手が同封してありますのでご注意ください。

Please (　　　　) (　　　　) (　　　　) (　　　　) is enclosed herewith.

3 without notice ／ 予告なしに

価格は予告なしに変更されることがある。

Prices are subject to (　　　　) (　　　　) (　　　　).

4 without permission ／ 許可なく

著作権のあるものをネットに無断で載せることはできない。

You can't put copyrighted material (　　　　) (　　　　) (　　　　).

GRAMMAR AND USAGE TO REMEMBER 例文を和訳してみよう。

1 心理状態を表す助動詞

🐾 動詞を助ける「助動詞」は〈助動詞＋動詞の原形 (do)〉という形で，動詞に話し手の心持ちをつけ加える。

🐾 心理状態を表す助動詞には，「意志」を表す will [shall] (〜するつもりである)，「許可・禁止」を表す may [can] (〜してもよい)，must not (〜してはいけない)，「能力・可能」を表す can (〜することができる)，could (〜することができた)，「推量・可能性」を表す may [might] (〜するかもしれない)，must (〜に違いない)，can (〜しかねない)，cannot (〜のはずがない)，「義務・意志」を表す must (〜しなければならない)，should (〜すべきだ)，「必要」を表す need (〜する必要がある)，「提案・勧誘」を表す Shall I? (私が〜しましょうか？)，Shall we? (いっしょに〜しませんか？) などがある。

例1 ▶ Too much exercise *can* be harmful to your health.

［推量・可能性の can］

🐾 心理状態を表す助動詞を2つつなげて，話し手の心理を2つ同時に表現することはできないので，can や must の代わりに，助動詞を同じ働きをする be able to や have to を用いて，will be able to や will have to と表現する。

例2 ▶ You *will be able to get* the book on the Internet.
[⟨will be able to *do*⟩]

---

2 助動詞と同じ働きをする語句

🐾 助動詞と同じ働きをする語句には，*be* able to（〜できる），have to（〜しなければならない），don't have to（〜する必要はない），had better（〜するほうがよい），had better not（〜しないほうがよい），may well（〜するのももっともだ），ought to（〜すべきである；〜するはずだ），ought not to（〜すべきでない），used to（以前は〜だった；よく〜したものだ），would rather（むしろ〜したい）などがある。

例3 ▶ Which country *would* you *rather* go to? ［⟨would rather *do*⟩］

---

3 ⟨助動詞＋ have ＋過去分詞⟩

🐾 ⟨助動詞＋ have ＋過去分詞（*done*）⟩には，過去のことがらに対する「推量」を表す must have *done*（〜したに違いない），may [might] have *done*（〜したかもしれない），can't [couldn't] have *done*（〜したはずがない），過去のことがらに対する「後悔・非難」を表す should [ought to] have *done*（〜すべきだったのに），shouldn't [ought not to] have *done*（〜すべきでなかったのに），need not have *done*（〜する必要はなかったのに）などがある。

例4 ▶ He *may have missed* the train. ［⟨may have *done*⟩］

例5 ▶ Thank you, but you *needn't have bought* me a present.
［⟨need not have *done*⟩］

マンガを和訳してみよう

【やぶへび！】

🐾 過去のことがらに対する「後悔・非難」を表す〈助動詞＋have＋過去分詞〉shouldn't have *done* は「〜すべきでなかったのに」という意味を表す。

① Hey, stupid cat!　How do you like my new wastebasket?

_____

② Please feel free to use it if you have something to throw away.

_____

③ I shouldn't have suggested it.

_____

A カッコ内の適当なものを選んでみよう。

1. もし雨がやめば，私たちはテニスをすることができる。

   We'll (be able to / can) play tennis if it stops raining.

2. 台風が来ているので，今日は外出しないほうがいいよ。

   The typhoon is coming, so you'd (better not / not better) go out today.

3. メールの返事を出さなかったので，彼女は怒っているに違いない。

   She (must / would rather) be angry because I didn't reply to her email.

B 日本文を英語に直してみよう。

1. 家に帰る途中でこの手紙をポストに入れて (mail) おきましょうか?

   _____?

2. 私の兄は若いころマラソン (marathons) を走ることができた。

   _____.

3. 子どものころよくおじいちゃん (my grandad) と釣りに行ったものだ。

   _____.

C カッコ内の語句を並べかえて，英文を完成させてみよう。

1. ニューヨークの新居はどうですか? (How do you like A?)

   How [in / do / house / like / new / New York / you / your]?

   _____?

2. 彼にお金を貸すのはまるで捨てるようなものだ。(throw A away)

   Lending [away / just like / him / is / it / money / throwing].

   _____.

3. 冷蔵庫に入っているものを何でも自由に食べてね。(feel free to *do*)

Feel [anything ／ free ／ help ／ in ／ the refrigerator ／ to ／ to ／ yourself].

_____.

D 下線部に入る最も適当なものを選んでみよう。

1. I _____ have made more friends when I was a college student.

    (A) must　　**(B)** need not　　**(C)** should

2. The hotel list in this brochure is tentative, and _____ be changed without notice.

    (A) may　　**(B)** need　　**(C)** would rather

3. The materials that were distributed yesterday _____ be copied without permission.

    (A) be able to　　**(B)** must not　　**(C)** used to

E 下線部に入る最も適当なものを選んでみよう。

1. When entering the building, you _____ insert an authorization card into an input device on the door.

    (A) cannot　　**(B)** could　　**(C)** must　　**(D)** shall

2. Please note that we will not _____ accept any application or resume submitted after the due date.

    (A) be able to　　**(B)** don't have to　　**(C)** had better　　**(D)** would rather

3. The band that we hired for the party has canceled, so we will _____ find another band by next week.

    (A) can　　**(B)** have to　　**(C)** must　　**(D)** should

Unit 11

主語と動詞の一致
SUBJECT-VERB AGREEMENT

LET'S LEARN

WORDS TO REMEMBER 語群・頭文字をヒントにカッコを埋めてみよう。

（1） 海賊 　（　　　　　　　　　　　　　）

（2） 患者 　（　　　　　　　　　　　　　）

（3） きわめて 　（　　　　　　　　　　　　　）

（4） 余分な 　（　　　　　　　　　　　　）

（5） ～を開発する 　（　　　　　　　　　　　　）

（6） ～を発生させる 　（　　　　　　　　　　　　）

（7） 効果がある 　（ e　　　　　　　　　　）

（8） 出版社 　（ p　　　　　　　　　　）

（9） 意見 　（ r　　　　　　　　　）

（10） 糖尿病患者 　（ d　　　　　　　　　　　）

［語群］

《 develop ／ excess ／ extremely ／ generate ／ patient ／ pirate 》

EXPRESSIONS TO REMEMBER カッコを埋めて英文を完成させてみよう。

1 enable A to *do* ／ A が ～できるようにする

そのソフトのおかげで，私たちはその仕事を短時間で終えることができた。

The software (　　　　　　　　　　　　　　　　　　　　　　　　　　）

in a short time.

2 import A from B ／ A を B から輸入する［導入する］

日本はブラジルからコーヒーを輸入している。

Japan (　　　　　　　　　　　　　　　　　　　　　　　　　　　）.

3 prove to be C ／ Cであることがわかる

彼女の意見は正しいことがわかった。

Her remarks (   ).

4 sell A to B ／ AをBに売る

君は本を書いて出版社に売るといいよ。

You should write a book and (

).

 GRAMMAR AND USAGE TO REMEMBER 例文を和訳してみよう。

1 動名詞の主語

🐾 動名詞の主語は単数形の動詞で受ける。

例1 ▶ Discussing things in English *is* quite difficult for Japanese students. ［動名詞が主語］

_____

2 〈There [Here]＋動詞＋主語〉構文

🐾 〈There [Here]＋動詞＋主語〉構文では，動詞は主語に合わせる。

例2 ▶ There *are* some things money can't buy. ［some thingsが主語］

_____

3 all of A ／ most of A ／ some of A

🐾 〈all of A〉（Aのすべて），〈most of A〉（Aのほとんど），〈some of A〉（Aのいくつか［いくらか］）が主語の場合，動詞はAに一致させる。

4 a number of A ／ the number of A

🐾 〈a number of A〉（多くのA）が主語の場合，複数形の動詞で受け，〈the number of A〉（Aの数）が主語の場合，単数形の動詞で受ける。

例3 ▶ A number of people *were* burned out by the fire. ［〈a number of A〉］

_____

例4 ▶ What *was* the number of students enrolled last year?
[〈the number of A〉]

⑤ 相関語句

- 〈both A and B〉(AもBも両方)が主語の場合，動詞は複数形の動詞で受け，〈either A or B〉(AとBのどちらか)や〈neither A nor B〉(AでもなくBでもない)が主語の場合，動詞はBに一致させ，〈A as well as B〉(BだけでなくAもまた)，〈A rather than B〉(BよりもむしろA)が主語の場合，動詞は意味の中心となるAに一致させる。

例5 ▶ Neither the teacher nor the students *were* in the hall.
[〈neither A nor B〉]

⑥ 単数形の動詞で受けるもの

- 学問名 (economics「経済学」, mathematics「数学」)・学科名・ゲーム名・国名 (the Philippines「フィリピン」)・新聞名・雑誌名・news (知らせ；ニュース) などは単数形の動詞で受ける。

例6 ▶ Billiards *is* an extremely complex game. ［ゲーム名］

⑦ 複数形の動詞で受けるもの

- pants (ズボン), glasses (メガネ) のように，対を成す部分から成る衣類や道具，clothes (衣服), goods (商品) などは複数形の動詞で受ける。

例7 ▶ These *scissors* cut well, ［対を成す部分から成る道具］

LET'S READ

マンガを和訳してみよう

【何も見えない！】

🐾 〈Here＋be動詞＋主語〉構文ではbe動詞は主語に合わせる。

＊Conrad 「コンラッド」 スヌーピーのビーグル・スカウトのメンバー。雨ごいダンスで雨を降らすことができる。

＊Blackbeagle 「ブラック・ビーグル」 スヌーピーの海賊名。

＊lead A ashore 「Aをひきいて上陸する」

＊scurvy 「卑劣な」

① A pirate ship!　I see a pirate ship!

_____

② Here's Blackbeagle, the world famous pirate, leading his scurvy band ashore.

_____

③ ……

④ Somebody tell Conrad he's only supposed to wear one eye patch.

BONK!

_____

A カッコ内の適当なものを選んでみよう。

1. 製造コストの削減は，私たちが考えるべき主要素である。

   Reducing production costs (are / is) the key factor we have to consider.

2. 最近，この町の自動車事故の数は減少している。

   The number of car accidents in this city (are / has been) decreasing recently.

3. 氷山は水面に出ている部分はごくわずかで，大部分が水面下にある。

   Only a part of an iceberg shows above water; most of it (are / is) under water.

B be動詞でカッコを埋めて英文を完成させてみよう。

1. 商品が到着するのが遅れたらどうすればいいのでしょうか？

   What should I do if the goods (　　　　　　) delivered late?

2. 彼女が必要としているのは，お金より友だちだ。

   Friends, rather than money, (　　　　　　) what she needs.

3. 経済学は現代の大学での中心的な学問である。

   Economics (　　　　　　) a core discipline in the modern university.

C カッコ内の語句を並べかえて，英文を完成させてみよう。

1. これをあげましょう。(Here is A)

   Here [something / a / for / is / little / you].

   _____.

2. リサはいつもジーンズとTシャツを着ている。(wear A)

   Lisa [a / always / and / jeans / T-shirt / wears].

   _____.

3. その質問をきっかけに先生は長い文法説明を始めた。(lead A into B)

The question [a / explanation / into / grammatical / led / long / the teacher].

_____

_____.

D 下線部に入る最も適当なものを選んでみよう。

1. Both eating right and exercising regularly _____ reduce excess weight.

    (A) has helped   **(B)** help   **(C)** helps

2. Some of the electricity generated in this power plant _____ sold to other states.

    (A) are   **(B)** have been   **(C)** is

3. All of the company's products _____ made from oil, which is mostly imported from Saudi Arabia.

    (A) are   **(B)** has been   **(C)** is

E 下線部に入る最も適当なものを選んでみよう。

1. The number of diabetics to whom the newly developed medicine has proved to be effective _____ still limited.

    (A) are   **(B)** have been   **(C)** is   **(D)** was

2. Thanks to high pressure covering this region throughout the month, there _____ very little storm activity on the western coast.

    (A) have been   **(B)** is   **(C)** was   **(D)** were

3. Software developed recently by our company, which enables patients to contact medical professionals over the Internet, _____ a lot of attention.

    (A) are gaining   **(B)** gain   **(C)** has gained   **(D)** have gained

Unit 12

受動態
PASSIVE VOICE

LET'S LEARN

WORDS TO REMEMBER 語群・頭文字をヒントにカッコを埋めてみよう。

（1） 寄贈者 （　　　　　　　　　　）

（2） 収集する価値のある （　　　　　　　　　　　）

（3） 慈善団体 （　　　　　　　　　）

（4） 相当な （　　　　　　　　）

（5） タコ （　　　　　　　　　）

（6） 日帰りの （　　　　　　　　）

（7） 心地よい （ c　　　　　　　　　　）

（8） 奨学金 （ s　　　　　　　　）

（9） 乗客 （ p　　　　　　　　）

（10） 匿名の （ a　　　　　　　　　）

[語群]

《 charity ／ collectable ／ considerable ／ donor ／ octopus ／ same-day 》

EXPRESSIONS TO REMEMBER カッコを埋めて英文を完成させてみよう。

1 apply for A ／ Aを申請する

私は奨学金を申請した。

I have (　　　　　　　　　　　　　　　　　　　　　).

2 contribute A to B ／ AをBに寄付する

彼はその慈善団体に多額のお金を寄付した。

He (　　　　　　　　　　　　　　　　　　　　　)

the charity.

③ encourage A to *do* ／ Aに～するよう推奨する

学生たちはリンカーンの伝記を読むことを勧められた。

The students (   )

of Lincoln.

④ reserve A for B ／ AをBのために予約する

彼女のために博多までの列車の席を予約した。

I (   ) on

the train to Hakata.

 GRAMMAR AND USAGE TO REMEMBER　例文を和訳してみよう。

① 受動態

　　🐾 「動作を行うもの」を主語にした表現を「能動態」といい，「動作を受けるもの」を主語にした表現を「受動態」という。

例1 ▶　Bell *invented* the telephone.　［能動態］

_____

例2 ▶　The telephone *was invented* by Bell.　［受動態］

_____

　　🐾 受動態は〈be動詞＋他動詞の過去分詞（＋by＋動作主）〉の形で表される。

例3 ▶　*Winnie-the-Pooh is loved by* many people around the world.

_____

　　🐾 動作主があまり重要でない受動態では，〈by＋動作主〉がよく省略される。

　　🐾 受動態の時制には，現在形〈is [are, am]＋過去分詞〉，過去形〈was [were]＋過去分詞〉，未来形〈will be＋過去分詞〉，進行形〈is [are, am, was, were] being＋過去分詞〉，完了形〈have [has, had] been＋過去分詞〉がある。

例4 ▶　A new stadium *is being built* for the Olympics.　［進行形］

_____

2 〈be 動詞以外の動詞＋過去分詞〉

🐾 〈be 動詞＋過去分詞〉の受動態は「動作」（～される；～られる）と「状態」（～されている；～られている）の両方の意味を表すため，「動作」の意味を明確にするために，be 動詞の代わりに get や become を，「状態」の意味を明確にするために，be 動詞の代わりに remain や lie を用いることがある。

例5 ▶ The treasure *lay hidden* in the island for years.　［「状態」を表す lie］

---

3 by 以外の前置詞を用いる受動態

🐾 by 以外の前置詞を用いる受動態には，*be* caught in ～（～に偶然あう），*be* covered with ～（～におおわれている），*be* derived from ～（～に由来する），*be* disappointed at ～（～に失望する），*be* interested in ～（～に興味がある），*be* known for ～（～で知られている），*be* known to ～（～に知られている），*be* satisfied with ～（～に満足している），*be* worried about ～（～が心配である）などがある。

例6 ▶ He *is* very much *interested in* astronomy.　［〈*be* interested in ～〉］

---

4 「受け身」を表す注意すべき表現

🐾 「受け身」を表す注意すべき表現には，well などの副詞とともに用いられて受け身を表す cut（切れる），sell（売れる），wash（洗える）などと，「～される」「～してもらう」という意味を表す〈have [get] ＋目的語＋過去分詞〉がある。

例7 ▶ His new book is *selling* well.　［sell（売れる）］

マンガを和訳してみよう

【大親友は何でも知っている！】

🐾　get caught は「動作」を表す受動態。

＊ if we wanted to (fly) 「もし望めば」　if を用いて現在の事実と反対を表す仮定法過去。

① Dogs could fly if we wanted to.

_____

② ……

③ You're right.　Our collars would get caught in the trees.

_____

④ How did you know that?

_____

LET'S TRY

A カッコ内の適当なものを選んでみよう。

1. 私は試験の結果に満足している。

   I'm satisfied (at / with) my exam results.

2. 京都は古いお寺や神社で知られている。

   Kyoto is known (for / to) its old temples and shrines.

3. 彼はお祭りのときにスリにあった。

   He had his pocket (picked / picking) during the festival.

B カッコ内の語を並べかえて，英文を完成させてみよう。

1. Green tea [be / for / good / health / is / said / to / your].

   _____.

2. Many flights [because / canceled / have / of / the / typhoon / been].

   _____

   _____.

3. The documents [a / are / copied / minute / now, / please / so / wait / being].

   _____

   _____.

C カッコ内の語句を並べかえて，英文を完成させてみよう。

1. 私は家に帰る途中ににわか雨にあった。(get done)

   I [caught / got / home / in / on / the shower / the way].

   _____.

2. 大きくなったら何になりたい？（want to *do*）

What [be ／ do ／ grow ／ to ／ up ／ want ／ when ／ you ／ you]?

_____?

3. 彼のアドレスを知っていれば，連絡をとることができるのに。（ifを用いた仮定法過去）

If [address, ／ contact ／ could ／ email ／ him ／ his ／ I ／ I ／ knew].

_____.

D 下線部に入る最も適当なものを選んでみよう。

1. The word "octopus" is derived _____ the Latin word meaning "eight-footed."

   (A) at   **(B)** from   **(C)** to

2. A wonderful antique chair was _____ to the museum by an anonymous donor.

   (A) contribute   **(B)** contributed   **(C)** contributing

3. Collectable items from old stadium will _____ online from 7 P.M. next Monday.

   (A) be selling   **(B)** be sold   **(C)** sell

E 下線部に入る最も適当なものを選んでみよう。

1. Mail carriers _____ to wear comfortable shoes as their work involves considerable walking.

   (A) are encouraged   **(B)** has been encouraged
   (C) have encouraged   **(D)** encourage

2. The lounges on the third floor _____ for first-class passengers with a same-day return ticket.

   (A) are reserved   **(B)** has been reserved   **(C)** is reserving   **(D)** reserved

3. To apply for a patent, several countries still require that all documents _____ into their own languages.

   (A) be translated   **(B)** is being translated
   (C) translated   **(D)** will be translating

Unit 13

不定詞
INFINITIVES

WORDS TO REMEMBER 語群・頭文字をヒントにカッコを埋めてみよう。

(1) 応募者　（　　　　　　　　　　　　　）

(2) 賢明な　（　　　　　　　　　　　　　）

(3) 販売店　（　　　　　　　　　　　　　）

(4) 複雑な　（　　　　　　　　　　　　　）

(5) 〜を断る　（　　　　　　　　　　　　）

(6) 〜を要求する　（　　　　　　　　　　　）

(7) 宇宙飛行士　（ a　　　　　　　　　　　）

(8) 好み　（ p　　　　　　　　　）

(9) 野球場　（ b　　　　　　　　）

(10) 正規の　（ r　　　　　　　　　　　）

［語群］

《 applicant ／ complex ／ dealership ／ reject ／ require ／ wise 》

EXPRESSIONS TO REMEMBER カッコを埋めて英文を完成させてみよう。

1 as C as possible ／ できるだけCに

彼らはできるだけ速く走った。

They (　　　　　　　　　　　　　　　　　　　　　　).

2 at the latest ／ 遅くとも

レポートは遅くとも次の金曜日までに提出のこと。

You must submit your paper (

　　　　　　　　　　　　).

3 *be* late for A ／ Aに遅刻する

彼女とのデートに20分遅刻した。

I (　　　　　　　　　　　　　　　　　　　　　　　　　　　　　) a date
with her.

4 bring A to B ／ AをBに持って行く

パーティーには何を持って行ったらいい？

What should (　　　　　　　　　　　　　　　　　　　　　　　)?

 GRAMMAR AND USAGE TO REMEMBER 例文を和訳してみよう。

1 to不定詞

🐾 不定詞には，〈to＋動詞の原形〉の「to不定詞」とtoのない「原形不定詞」がある。

🐾 to不定詞はその働きによって，「名詞的用法」(「〜すること」「〜であること」という意味をもち，文中で主語・補語・目的語として働く)，「形容詞的用法」(「〜するための」という意味をもち，後ろから名詞・代名詞を修飾する)，「副詞的用法」(「目的」「原因・理由」「判断の根拠」「結果」「条件」などの意味をもち，動詞，形容詞，副詞，文全体などを修飾する) がある。

例1 ▶ My dream is *to become* an astronaut. ［名詞的用法／補語］

_____

🐾 to不定詞の意味上の主語は，to不定詞の前に〈for＋意味上の主語〉を置いて表す。

🐾 to不定詞の否定形はnotやneverといった否定語をその直前に置く。

2 原形不定詞

🐾 toのない原形不定詞は，〈知覚動詞 (feel, hear, listen to, look at, see, watchなど)＋目的語＋原形不定詞〉と〈使役動詞 (have, let, make)＋目的語＋原形不定詞〉という構文で用いられる。これらの用法において，〈目的語＋原形不定詞〉は意味の上で〈主語＋述語〉の関係にある。

例2 ▶ I felt the floor *move* and saw the walls *shake*. ［知覚動詞］

_____

3 to不定詞のみを目的語にとる動詞

🐾 to不定詞のみを目的語にとる動詞には, decide〜（〜を決める）, expect〜（〜を期待する）, hesitate〜（〜をためらう）, hope〜（〜を望む）, plan〜（〜を計画する）, pretend〜（〜のふりをする）, promise〜（〜を約束する）などがある。

例3 ▶ Don't hesitate *to ask* me if you want anything.

［to不定詞のみを目的語にとる動詞］

---

4 to不定詞を含む注意すべき表現

🐾 to不定詞を含む注意すべき表現には, It is C [A] (for B) to *do*（(Bが)〜するのはC [A] だ）, It is C (careless, kind, rude, wise などの人を評価する形容詞) of A to *do*（Aが〜するのはCだ）,〈疑問詞＋to不定詞〉,〈動詞＋目的語＋to不定詞〉(ask A to *do*「Aに〜するよう求める」, request A to *do*「Aに〜するよう頼む」, require A to *do*「Aに〜するよう要求する」など), 独立不定詞 (to tell the truth「実を言うと」, to begin with「まず最初に」, to be frank with you「率直に言うと」など), too C to *do*（あまりにもCなので〜できない）, C enough to *do*（〜するのに十分にC）などがある。

例4 ▶ *It was* careless *of you to leave* the door unlocked.

［〈It is C of A to *do*〉］

【かわいい!?】

> 🐾 ask A to do は〈動詞＋目的語＋to不定詞〉の構文。It must be a nice change to be served は〈It is A to do〉の形式主語構文。

① Your master is gone for the day so he asked me to feed you.

_____

② Actually, it must be a nice change to be served by a cute waitress.

_____

③ Define "cute."

_____

A カッコ内の適当なものを選んでみよう。

1. その子はあまりにも眠かったので，それ以上歩けなかった。

   The kid was (so / too) sleepy to walk any more.

2. 誰かが後ろから私の名前を呼ぶのが聞こえた。

   I heard someone (call / called) my name from behind.

3. あなたが自分の将来について考えることは大切だ。

   It is important (for / of) you to think about your future.

B 日本文を英語に直してみよう。

1. 私は新しいスマートフォンを買うために貯金している (saving money)。

   _____.

2. 実を言うと，そのことはあまりよく (much about～) 知らない。

   _____.

3. ルーシーの誕生日に (for her birthday) 何をあげればいいかわからない。

   _____.

C カッコ内の語句を並べかえて，英文を完成させてみよう。

1. 彼女は私たちをちらっと見て行ってしまった。(*be* gone)

   She [a glance / and then / gave / gone / she / us / was].

   _____.

2. チャックはお父さんに野球場に連れて行ってほしいと頼んだ。(ask A to *do*)

   Chuck [asked / father / him / his / take / the ballpark / to / to].

   _____.

3.　晴れた日に自転車に乗るのはとても楽しい。(It is A to *do*)

It [a bicycle ／ a great ／ a sunny ／ is ／ day ／ on ／ pleasure ／ ride ／ to].

_____.

D 下線部に入る最も適当なものを選んでみよう。

1.　You should avoid _____ antibiotics unless they are necessary.

(A) taking　　**(B)** to take　　**(C)** took

2.　The boss decided _____ the applicant only because he was late for the interview.

(A) rejected　　**(B)** rejecting　　**(C)** to reject

3.　When making an online flight booking, passengers are requested _____ their meal preferences.

(A) specified　　**(B)** specifying　　**(C)** to specify

E 下線部に入る最も適当なものを選んでみよう。

1.　Nurses today must be technically skilled enough _____ the complex machinery used in hospitals.

(A) operate　　**(B)** operated　　**(C)** operating　　**(D)** to operate

2.　It is the job of cabin attendants to make passengers _____ as comfortable as possible during the flight.

(A) feel　　**(B)** feeling　　**(C)** felt　　**(D)** to feel

3.　It was wise _____ you to bring your vehicle to a registered dealership when the need for professional repairs arose.

(A) for　　**(B)** of　　**(C)** to　　**(D)** with

Unit 14

動名詞
GERUNDS

WORDS TO REMEMBER

語群・頭文字をヒントにカッコを埋めてみよう。

(1) 移住する　（　　　　　　　　　　　　）

(2) 可能性のある　（　　　　　　　　　　　　）

(3) 退職　（　　　　　　　　　　）

(4) 罰金　（　　　　　　　　　）

(5) 負担　（　　　　　　　　　）

(6) 眠らずに　（　　　　　　　　　　　）

(7) 花壇　（　f　　　　　　　　　）

(8) 最新の　（　l　　　　　　　　　）

(9) 雑草　（　w　　　　　　　　　）

(10) 都会の　（　u　　　　　　　　　）

[語群]

《 awake ／ burden ／ fine ／ potential ／ relocate ／ retirement 》

EXPRESSIONS TO REMEMBER

カッコを埋めて英文を完成させてみよう。

1 *be* subject to A ／ Aを受けやすい

都会で働く人々はストレスがたまりやすい。

Urban workers (　　　　　　　　　　　　　　　　　　　　　　).

2 keep A C ／ AをCにしておく

彼女は足が冷えないようにウールの靴下をはいた。

She wore woolen socks (　　　　　　　　　　

　　　　　　　　　　　).

3 send A to B ／ A を B に送る

私たちに最新のカタログを送ってください。

Please (   ).

4 those who 〜 ／ 〜する人々

コンテストに参加したい方はこの用紙に記入してください。

(   ) part in the contest must fill out this form.

 GRAMMAR AND USAGE TO REMEMBER　例文を和訳してみよう。

1 動名詞

🐾 「動名詞」は、〈動詞の原形＋-ing〉の形で「〜すること」という意味を表し、動詞的性質（目的語や補語を伴ったり、副詞（句）によって修飾される）と名詞的性質（文中で主語・補語・目的語になる）を兼ね備えている。

🐾 動名詞の意味上の主語を表す必要がある場合には、ふつうその直前に所有格で示すが、目的格の場合もある。

例1 ▶ Do you mind *my* [*me*] sitting here?　[〈所有格 [目的格] +動名詞〉]

_____

🐾 動名詞の否定形は not や never といった否定語をふつうその直前に置く。

例2 ▶ I'm sorry for *not answering* your email.　[〈否定語+動名詞〉]

_____

2 動名詞のみを目的語にとる動詞

🐾 動名詞のみを目的語にとる動詞には、appreciate 〜（〜をありがたく思う）、avoid 〜（〜を避ける）、consider 〜（〜を検討する）、enjoy 〜（〜を楽しむ）、finish 〜（〜を終える）、suggest 〜（〜を提案する）などがある。

例3 ▶ When you finish *doing* the dishes, please clean the room.
　　　[動名詞のみを目的語にとる動詞]

_____

3 to不定詞と動名詞の両方を目的語にとる動詞

🐾 to不定詞と動名詞の両方を目的語にとる動詞には，どちらを用いてもほぼ同じ意味のbegin〜（〜を始める），continue〜（〜を続ける），like〜（〜を好む），hate〜（〜をひどく嫌う），propose〜（〜を提案する），start〜（〜を始める）などがある。

🐾 to不定詞と動名詞の両方を目的語にとる動詞には，意味が異なり，to不定詞は「これからすること」を，動名詞は「すでにしたこと」を表すforget〜（〜を忘れる），regret〜（〜を後悔する），remember〜（〜を覚えている），try〜（〜をやってみる）などがある。

例4 ▶ Olivia regret *leaving* her child alone at home. ［「すでにしたこと」］

---

4 動名詞を含む注意すべき表現

🐾 動名詞を含む注意すべき表現には，*be* used to *doing*（〜するのに慣れている），*be* worth *doing*（〜する価値がある），feel like *doing*（〜したい気がする），keep [prevent] A from *doing*（Aが〜するのを妨げる），look forward to *doing*（〜するのを楽しみにしている），spend A (in) *doing*（Aを〜するのに費やす），There is no *doing*（〜することができない），What do you say to *doing*?（〜するのはいかがですか？）などがある。

例5 ▶ Sam *spent* the summer vacation *traveling* in Asian countries.
［動名詞を含む注意すべき表現］

マンガを和訳してみよう

【哲学者それとも不眠症!?】

🐾 keep my life from going by（人生が過ぎないようにする）の動名詞 going は前置詞 from の目的語。try slowing down（試しに減速してみる）の動名詞 slowing は動詞の目的語。

① Sometimes I lie awake at night, and I ask, "What can I do to keep my life from going by so fast?"

_____

_____

② Then a voice comes to me that says, "Try slowing down at the corners."

_____

A カッコ内の適当なものを選んでみよう。

1. コンサートの後，そのピアニストに会いたかったのですが。

   I had hoped (seeing / to see) the pianist after the concert.

2. そのメールをメンバー全員に忘れずに送ってください。

   Remember (sending / to send) the email to all the members.

3. 私は海岸沿いを走る毎朝の自転車通勤を楽しんでいる。

   I enjoy (commuting / to commute) by bicycle along the oceanfront every morning.

B 下線部を埋めて英文を完成させてみよう。

1. こんなに晴れた日には勉強する気にならない。

   I _____ on such a sunny day.

2. 私は試しにその番号に電話してみたが，誰も出なかった。

   I _____, but there was no answer.

3. 大雪のためにその飛行機は離陸できなかった。

   The heavy snow _____.

C カッコ内の語句を並べかえて，英文を完成させてみよう。

1. この犬に自分の家に入るのを妨げられた。（keep A from *doing*）

   I [by / dog / entering / home / kept / my own / this / was / from].

   _____.

2. モーターが動かなかったので彼女はバンとたたいてみた。(try *doing*)

Since [a bang / didn't / giving / she / start, / the motor / tried / it].

_____.

3. 年が経つうちに，私は次第にその出来事のことを忘れた。(go by)

As [about / by, / forgot / I gradually / the incident / the years / went].

_____.

D 下線部に入る最も適当なものを選んでみよう。

1. Studying abroad is a good way _____ a foreign language.

    (A) learning   **(B)** learned   **(C)** to learn

2. Flowerbeds can be kept neat and attractive by regularly _____ weeds.

    (A) removed   **(B)** removing   **(C)** to remove

3. I couldn't avoid _____ through the suburbs; the main road through the city was blocked.

    (A) driving   **(B)** drove   **(C)** to drive

E 下線部に入る最も適当なものを選んでみよう。

1. _____ a user-friendly Web site is one of the keys to attracting potential customers.

    (A) Create   **(B)** Creating   **(C)** Creation   **(D)** Creative

2. The new president sent an email to all employees saying that he looked forward _____ with them.

    (A) to work   **(B)** to working   **(C)** work   **(D)** working

3. My parents are considering _____ to a place with mild climates, attractive real estate prices, and lower tax burdens after retirement.

    (A) relocate   **(B)** relocated   **(C)** relocating   **(D)** to relocate

Unit 15

分詞
PARTICIPLES

LET'S LEARN

WORDS TO REMEMBER　語群・頭文字をヒントにカッコを埋めてみよう。

（1）　稲妻　（　　　　　　　　　　　）

（2）　注射　（　　　　　　　　　　　）

（3）　流れる　（　　　　　　　　　　）

（4）　部品　（　　　　　　　　　　）

（5）　有機的に　（　　　　　　　　　　）

（6）　〜を修理する　（　　　　　　　　　　）

（7）　行き先　（　d　　　　　　　　　）

（8）　化学物質　（　c　　　　　　　　　）

（9）　観光客　（　t　　　　　　　　　）

（10）　〜を栽培する　（　r　　　　　　　　　）

［語群］

《 lightning ／ organically ／ part ／ repair ／ run ／ shot 》

EXPRESSIONS TO REMEMBER　カッコを埋めて英文を完成させてみよう。

1　burn down A ／ Aを焼き尽す

　　稲妻による火災で数軒の家が全焼した。

　　A fire started by lightning (

　　　　　　　　　　　　　　　　　　　).

2　leave A C ／ AをCの状態にしておく

　　それは言わないでおいたほうがいいと思う。

　　I think it's (　　　　　　　　　　　　　　　　　　　　　　).

3 on time ／ 時間どおりに

列車はぴったり時間どおりに到着した。

The train ( ).

4 out of stock ／ 品切れで

申し訳ありませんが，この型の帽子はただ今品切れです。

I'm sorry, but hats in this style ( ).

GRAMMAR AND USAGE TO REMEMBER　例文を和訳してみよう。

1 分詞

🐾 「分詞」は，動詞でありながら形容詞としての働きをするもので「動作の進行」（～する；～している）を表す「現在分詞」（形は動名詞と同じ）と「完了した動作や出来事」（～される；～し（てしまっ）た）を表す「過去分詞」がある。

🐾 分詞の基本用法には，進行形〈be動詞＋現在分詞〉，完了形〈have [has, had]＋過去分詞〉，受動態〈be動詞＋過去分詞〉がある。

🐾 「感情」を表す分詞形容詞には，〈人〉と結びつく，amazed（驚いている），bored（退屈している），confused（当惑している），excited（興奮している），〈もの〉と結びつく，amazing（驚くべき），boring（退屈な），confusing（まぎらわしい），exciting（わくわくする）などがある。

2 分詞の限定用法

🐾 名詞を修飾する「分詞の限定用法」では，分詞が単独で名詞を修飾する場合には，その名詞の直前に置かれ，分詞が他の語句を伴って名詞を修飾する場合には，その名詞の直後に置かれる。

🐾 限定用法では「名詞と現在分詞」は意味上〈主語＋述語〉の能動関係になり，「過去分詞と名詞」は意味上〈述語＋目的語〉の受動関係になる。

例1 ▶ The language *spoken in Brazil* is Portuguese.　[分詞の限定用法]

_____

3 分詞の叙述用法

🐾 「分詞の叙述用法」には，主格補語になる用法〈主語＋動詞＋主格補語（＝分詞）〉[第2文型]と目的格補語になる用法〈主語＋動詞＋目的語＋目的格補語（＝分詞）〉[第5文型]がある。

例2 ▶　Who left the water *running*?　［分詞の叙述用法］

_____

④　分詞構文

🐾　「分詞構文」とは，分詞が〈接続詞＋主語＋動詞〉の働きをする構文である。意
味は「時」「理由」「譲歩」「付帯状況」（〈with ＋名詞・代名詞＋分詞〉「…が〜し
て［されて］いる状態で」）「条件」に分けられるが，その意味は文の前後関係
によって決まる。分詞構文は，文頭はもちろん，文中や文尾にくることも
ある。

例3 ▶　I stayed in bed, *reading* a book.　［「〜しながら」］

_____

🐾　分詞構文の否定形は〈not [never] ＋分詞〉で表す。

🐾　主節の主語と分詞の主語が異なる場合は，分詞の主語を残す（独立分詞構文）。

🐾　分詞構文を含む注意すべき表現には，judging from〜（〜から判断すると），
strictly speaking（厳密に言えば），talking [speaking] of〜（〜と言えば）など
がある。

例4 ▶　*Judging from* his accent, he must be from Australia.
　　　［〈judging from〜〉］

_____

LET'S READ

マンガを和訳してみよう

【ぼくにもいるよ!】

WHEN I'M OUT WALKING, I ALWAYS FEEL SAFER WITH MY DOG FOLLOWING RIGHT BEHIND..

I FEEL THE SAME WAY..

7-24

🐾　with my dog following（自分の犬がついてきて）は〈with ＋名詞＋現在分詞〉構文で「付帯状況」を表す。

＊ right behind 「すぐ後ろを」

① When I'm out walking, I always feel safer with my dog following right behind.

_____

② I feel the same way.

_____

LET'S TRY

A カッコ内の適当なものを選んでみよう。

1. 働く母親の数が増えている。

The number of (worked / working) mothers has been increasing.

2. 子どもたちは動物園でパンダを見て大喜びした。

The children were (excited / exciting) to see the pandas in the zoo.

3. 駅からオフィスまでの道はわかりづらいので地図が必要でしょう。

The route to our office from the station is (confused / confusing), so you will need a map.

B 分詞でカッコを埋めて英文を完成させてみよう。

1. 宇宙から見ると，地球は青いボールのように見える。

(   ) from space, the earth looks like a blue ball.

2. 旅行と言えば，今までに中国へ行ったことがありますか？

(   ) of traveling, have you ever been to China?

3. 混んだ電車で足を組んで座ってはいけない。

Don't sit with your legs (   ) on a crowded train.

C カッコ内の語句を並べかえて，英文を完成させてみよう。

1. 彼女は目を閉じて音楽を聞いた。(with A *done*)

She [closed / eyes / her / listened / music / to / with].

_____.

2. サリーはコーヒーを1杯飲んでくつろいだ気分になった。（feel C）

Sally [a ／ after ／ coffee ／ cup ／ felt ／ having ／ of ／ relaxed].

_____.

3. 彼女が財布を開けると数枚の硬貨が落ちた。（副詞 out）

When [coins ／ fell out ／ her ／ opened ／ purse, ／ several ／ she].

_____.

D 下線部に入る最も適当なものを選んでみよう。

1. The parts _____ to repair the machine are out of stock.

   (A) need   (B) needed   (C) needing

2. The fire burned down scores of houses, _____ more than fifty people homeless.

   (A) leave   (B) leaving   (C) left

3. Hawaii is a popular tourist destination, _____ by millions of tourists every year.

   (A) visit   (B) visited   (C) visiting

E 下線部に入る最も適当なものを選んでみよう。

1. Employees _____ to have a flu shot should sign up in advance at the health center.

   (A) wish   (B) wished   (C) wishes   (D) wishing

2. Though _____ twenty minutes behind the schedule, the flight arrived at Narita on time.

   (A) being left   (B) having been left   (C) having left   (D) left

3. The company only sells vegetables and fruits _____ organically, without chemicals of any kind.

   (A) raise   (B) raised   (C) raising   (D) were raised

Unit 16

前置詞
PREPOSITIONS

LET'S LEARN

WORDS TO REMEMBER 語群・頭文字をヒントにカッコを埋めてみよう。

（1） 荒れ模様の　（　　　　　　　　　　　　　）

（2） 緊急事態　（　　　　　　　　　　　）

（3） 提出　（　　　　　　　　　　）

（4） 守ること　（　　　　　　　　　　）

（5） 〜に知らせる　（　　　　　　　　　　　）

（6） 〜を宣言する　（　　　　　　　　　　　）

（7） 言語学　（ l 　　　　　　　　　）

（8） 豪華な　（ g 　　　　　　　　　）

（9） 心理学　（ p 　　　　　　　　　）

（10） 植民地　（ c 　　　　　　　　　）

［語群］

《 declare ／ emergency ／ inclement ／ notify ／ observance ／ submission 》

EXPRESSIONS TO REMEMBER カッコを埋めて英文を完成させてみよう。

1 ask if... ／ …かどうか尋ねる

彼は私たちが学生かと尋ねた。

He (　　　　　　　　　　　　　　　　　　　　　　　　　).

2 *be* delayed ／ 遅れる

濃霧のためその航空便は2時間遅れた。

The flight (　　　　　　　　　　　　　　　　　　　　　　)

owing to the dense fog.

3 *be* made up of A ／ A から成り立っている

水は水素と酸素から成り立っている。

Water (   ) and
oxygen.

4 *be* postponed ／ 延期になる

その試合は大雨のため火曜日まで延期になった。

The game (   )
because of heavy rain.

 GRAMMAR AND USAGE TO REMEMBER 例文を和訳してみよう。

1 「場所」を表す前置詞

- 🐾 名詞や代名詞の前に置かれる「前置詞」は〈前置詞＋(代)名詞〉という形で，文中の動詞や名詞を後ろから修飾し，副詞句や形容詞句として文にいろいろな意味をつけ加える。

- 🐾 「場所」を表す前置詞には, at (〜に [地点・狭い場所]), in (〜に [広い場所]；〜の中に), on (〜に [接触]), from (〜から [出発点]), to (〜まで [到着点]), beside (〜の隣に [besides (〜のほかに)]), along (〜に沿って) などがある。

例1 ▶ There is a famous cake shop *beside* the bookstore. [「〜の隣に」]

_____

2 「時」を表す前置詞

- 🐾 「時」を表す前置詞には, at (〜に [時刻・時の一点]), in (〜に [月・季節・年・午前午後]), on (〜に [曜日・日・特定の午前午後]), from (〜から), to (〜まで), since (〜以来), till [until] (〜まで [継続]), by (〜までには [完了]), in (〜たつと), within (〜以内に), for (〜の間 [後ろには数字]), during (〜の間に；〜の間中 [後ろには特定の期間]), around (〜ぐらい), toward (〜ごろ) などがある。

例2 ▶ Emmy was born early *on* the morning of June 8. [特定の午前]

_____

3 その他の前置詞

🐾 「原因・理由」を表す前置詞には, for (〜のために), from (〜から) などが,「結果」を表す前置詞には, into (「変化」を表す), to (「到着点」を表す) などが,「分離」を表す前置詞には, of (〜から離れて), off (〜からはずれて) などが,「場所・範囲」を表す前置詞には, between (〜の間に [２つのもの]), among (〜の間に [３つ以上の同種のもの]) などがある。

例3 ▶ The art museum is famous *for* its gorgeous collection.
[「〜のために」]

4 群前置詞

🐾 「群前置詞」には, ２語から成る, according to〜 (〜によれば), as for〜 (〜について言えば), because of〜 (〜が原因で), due to〜 (〜のために), instead of〜 (〜の代わりに), owing to〜 (〜のために), thanks to〜 (〜のおかげで), ３語から成る, by means of〜 (〜によって), in addition to〜 (〜に加えて), in case of〜 (〜の場合には), in front of〜 (〜の前に), in spite of〜 (〜にもかかわらず), on account of〜 (〜のために) などがある。

例4 ▶ Why don't you do something *instead* of complaining?
[群前置詞「〜の代わりに」]

例5 ▶ *In addition to* Japanese, Karen can speak Chinese and Korean.
[群前置詞「〜に加えて」]

【暇つぶし！】

🐾　to（〜まで［到着点］），in（〜の中に），at（〜に［点］）は「場所」を表す前置詞。

＊ ma'am「先生」

① No, ma'am.　He's not my dog.

　_____

② He just followed me to school.

　_____

③ I think she wants to know why you're here in kindergarten.

　_____

④ I looked at my calendar, and saw I had a free day.

　_____

A カッコ内の適当なものを選んでみよう。

1. 大通りには素敵なレストランがいくつかある。

   There are some nice restaurants (in ／ on) the main street.

2. その仕事は週末までに完成すべきだ。

   The task should be completed (by ／ until) the end of the week.

3. 聖書によると，神は6日間で世界を創造されたそうだ。

   (According to ／ Due to) the Bible, God created the world in six days.

B 日本文を英語に直してみよう。

1. 両親のおかげで，私は大学に行くことができた。

   _____ .

2. 2つの計画の間の相違を説明させてください (Let me *do*)。

   _____ .

3. 私はロンドン滞在中に数か所の (several) 博物館を訪れた。

   _____ .

C カッコ内の語句を並べかえて，英文を完成させてみよう。

1. マイケルはフェンスを飛び越え，私も続いて飛び越えた。(follow A)

   Michael [him ／ and ／ followed ／ I ／ jumped ／ the fence ／ over].

   _____ .

2. なぜ外国語を習わなければならないかわかりません。(know why…)

   I [a ／ don't ／ foreign language ／ have ／ I ／ know ／ learn ／ to ／ why].

   _____ .

3. 彼は私に目を向けたけど，私だということに気づかなかったと思うわ。(look at A)

He [at / but I / don't / he / looked / me / me, / recognized / think].

_____.

D 下線部に入る最も適当なものを選んでみよう。

1. She has a doctor's degree in psychology _____ one in linguistics.

    (A) along   **(B)** beside   **(C)** besides

2. The thirteen colonies declared their independence from England _____ 1776.

    (A) at   **(B)** in   **(C)** on

3. _____ the inclement weather, all of the day's flights were delayed or canceled.

    (A) As for   **(B)** Due to   **(C)** In spite of

E 下線部に入る最も適当なものを選んでみよう。

1. _____ emergency, please call the number listed in the manual to notify our staff.

    (A) According to   **(B)** Because of   **(C)** By means of   **(D)** In case of

2. Ms. Smith called to ask if the deadline for submission for the draft could be postponed _____ after midnight.

    (A) by   **(B)** for   **(C)** since   **(D)** until

3. In neighborhoods made up of young adults, families, and senior citizens, the observance of the rules is key to creating harmony _____ residents.

    (A) among   **(B)** between   **(C)** to   **(D)** under

接続詞
CONJUNCTIONS

LET'S LEARN

WORDS TO REMEMBER
語群・頭文字をヒントにカッコを埋めてみよう。

（1） 栄養価が高い 　（　　　　　　　　　　　　）

（2） 習慣となる 　（　　　　　　　　　　　）

（3） 主要な 　（　　　　　　　　　　）

（4） 獣医 　（　　　　　　　　　　）

（5） ～を漏らす 　（　　　　　　　　　　　）

（6） 費用がかかる 　（　　　　　　　　　　　　）

（7） キャンプ場 　（　c　　　　　　　　　　）

（8） 個人 　（　i　　　　　　　　　）

（9） 物質 　（　m　　　　　　　　　　）

（10） 有機栽培による 　（　o　　　　　　　　　　　）

［語群］

《 addictive ／ costly ／ major ／ nutritious ／ reveal ／ vet 》

EXPRESSIONS TO REMEMBER
カッコを埋めて英文を完成させてみよう。

❶ *be* accompanied by A ／ A が付き添っている

少女には母親が付き添っていた。

The little girl (　　　　　　　　　　　　　　　　　　　　　　　).

❷ *be* aware of A ／ A に気づいている

彼女は知らず知らずのうちに秘密を漏らしてしまっていた。

She had revealed the secret (　　　　　　　　　　　

　　　　　　　　　).

3 C one ／ C なもの

彼の中古車は私の新車より値段が高かった。

His used car was ( ).

4 the cost of A ／ A の値段

近ごろガソリンの値段が高い。

( ) nowadays.

GRAMMAR AND USAGE TO REMEMBER 例文を和訳してみよう。

1 等位接続詞

🐾 語と語，句と句，節と節を接続する語を「接続詞」という。接続詞には，「等位接続詞」と「従位接続詞」がある。

🐾 語句や節を対等な関係でつなぐ等位接続詞には，〜and ... （〜と…；〜そして…），〜but ... （〜だが…；〜しかし…），〜or ... （〜または…；〜それとも…），so ... （そういうわけで…），for ... （というのは…だから）などがある。

🐾 等位接続詞を用いた慣用表現には，〈命令文＋and ...〉（〜しなさい，そうすれば…），〈命令文＋or ...〉（〜しなさい，さもないと…）などがある。

例1 ▶ Leave now, *and* you'll be in time for the train. ［〈命令文＋and ...〉］

_____

2 名詞節を導く従位接続詞

🐾 名詞節を導く従位接続詞には, that ... （…ということ；…という）, if [whether] ... （…かどうか）などがある。

例2 ▶ He went to the front door to see *if* it was locked.

［名詞節を導く従位接続詞］

_____

🐾 whether節が主語や補語の場合や〈名詞＋whether...〉,〈前置詞＋whether...〉,〈whether to *do*〉という構文ではifは使えない。

例3 ▶ *Whether* the patient will recover is uncertain. ［whether節が主語］

_____

3 副詞節を導く従位接続詞

🐾 副詞節を導く従位接続詞には,「時」を表す since…(…して以来), once…(いったん…したら), before…(…の前に),「原因・理由」を表す because…(…だから), as…(…なので),「条件」を表す if…(もし…なら), unless…(もし…でないなら),「譲歩」を表す though [although]…(…だけれども),「様態」を表す as…(…のように) などがある。

例4 ▶ I want to be a vet *because* I like animals. ［副詞節を導く従位接続詞］

_____

4 相関接続詞・群接続詞

🐾 相関接続詞には, both A and B (AもBも両方とも), either A or B (AかBかどちらか一方), not only A but (also) B (AだけでなくBも), so C that…(とてもCなので…), such (C) A that…(とても (Cな) Aなので…) などがある。

例5 ▶ The singer is *popular not only* in Korea *but also* in Japan.
［相関接続詞］

_____

🐾 群接続詞には, as long as…(…する限りは), as soon as…(…するとすぐに), even if…(たとえ…でも), in case…(…するといけないので), no matter who [how]…(誰が [どんなに] …しようとも) などがある。

例6 ▶ *No matter how* busy you are, you must eat lunch. ［群接続詞］

_____

マンガを和訳してみよう

【違うでしょ!】

🐾 if... (もし…なら) は「条件」を表す副詞節を導く従位接続詞。

＊ get a bite 「魚が食いつく」

① If I get a bite, you grab the net.

_____

② Now!

_____

③ ……

A カッコ内の適当なものを選んでみよう。

1. 雨が降るといけないからカサを持っていきなさいよ。

   Take an umbrella with you, just (even if / in case) it rains.

2. うちのコーヒーラウンジに販売機が設置されて以来, 約1年が経過している。

   It's been almost a year (since / though) the vending machine in our coffee lounge was installed.

3. 危険な状態ですので, この辺りは車の運転には特に注意してください。

   Use extra caution when driving in this area, (because / once) there are hazardous conditions.

B 接続詞でカッコを埋めて英文を完成させてみよう。

1. 紙を節約しなさい, さもないと森林が破壊されてしまいます。

   Save paper, (　　　　　　　) forests will be destroyed.

2. 問題は私たちが1週間でその仕事を終えられるかどうかだ。

   The problem is (　　　　　　　) we can finish the work in a week.

3. その日は誰もがアイスクリームを食べるほどの暑い日だった。

   It was (　　　　　　　) a hot day that everyone was eating ice cream.

C カッコ内の語句を並べかえて, 英文を完成させてみよう。

1. そのキャンディーバーを少しかじらせて。(名詞 bite)

   Let [a / candy bar / bite of / have / me / your].

   _____.

2. もし何もすることがないなら，帰宅していいよ。（接続詞 if …）

If [anything / don't / do, / go / have / home / may / to / you / you].

_____.

3. エルビス・プレスリーは60年代に若者の心をつかんだ。（grab A）

Elvis Presley [in / of / grabbed / people / the hearts / the 60's / young].

_____.

D 下線部に入る最も適当なものを選んでみよう。

1. Passengers must board before 3:40 _____ the cruise ship will leave at 4:00.

    (A) because   **(B)** that   **(C)** until

2. _____ you stay here, you have to obey my rules.

    (A) As long as   **(B)** Since   **(C)** Unless

3. _____ accompanied by their parents, individuals under the age of 18 cannot rent a campsite.

    (A) Though   **(B)** If   **(C)** Unless

E 下線部に入る最も適当なものを選んでみよう。

1. In most major cities, the cost of parking is so high _____ many people living there do not own cars.

    (A) if   **(B)** or   **(C)** that   **(D)** whether

2. Eating organic vegetables is more costly, _____ more nutritious than eating conventionally-grown ones.

    (A) and   **(B)** because   **(C)** but   **(D)** unless

3. Not only do most smokers know the danger of smoking, _____ they are also aware of the addictive nature of nicotine.

    (A) and   **(B)** but   **(C)** or   **(D)** that

Unit 18

関係詞
RELATIVES

LET'S LEARN

WORDS TO REMEMBER 語群・頭文字をヒントにカッコを埋めてみよう。

（1） 金髪の　（　　　　　　　　　　　　）

（2） 装置　（　　　　　　　　　　　　）

（3） 小冊子　（　　　　　　　　　　　）

（4） 病棟　（　　　　　　　　　　）

（5） 〜に影響を与える　（　　　　　　　　　　）

（6） 〜を提供する　（　　　　　　　　　　）

（7） 金庫　（ s　　　　　　　　　）

（8） 能力　（ a　　　　　　　　　）

（9） 未亡人　（ w　　　　　　　　　　）

（10） 〜を設置する　（ i　　　　　　　　　　）

[語群]

《 booklet ／ equipment ／ fair ／ influence ／ offer ／ ward 》

EXPRESSIONS TO REMEMBER カッコを埋めて英文を完成させてみよう。

1 how to *do* ／〜の仕方

　　ビルだけがこの金庫の開け方を知っている。

　　Only Bill knows (　　　　　　　　　　　　　　　　　　　).

2 Let me *do* ／ 私に〜させてください

　　お皿を洗うのを手伝わせてください。

　　(　　　　　　　　　　　　　　　　　　　　) the

　　dishes.

③ show A B ／ AにBを教える

駅へ行く道を教えてください。

Please (　　　　　　　　　　　　　　　) to the
station.

④ talk about A ／ Aについて話す

彼女はロサンゼルスでの自分の生活について話した。

She (　　　　　　　　　　　　　　　) Los
Angeles.

GRAMMAR AND USAGE TO REMEMBER　例文を和訳してみよう。

① 関係代名詞

- 名詞・代名詞の後ろに置かれ，その語に導かれる節を名詞・代名詞に関係づける「関係詞」には，「関係代名詞」と「関係副詞」がある。

- 2つの文をつなぐ〈接続詞＋代名詞〉の働きを併せもつ関係代名詞には，who（主格：[先行詞] 人），whose（所有格：[先行詞] 人・人以外），whom [who]（目的格：[先行詞] 人），which（主格・目的格：[先行詞] 人以外），of which（所有格：[先行詞] 人以外），that（主格・目的格：[先行詞] 人以外・人）などがある。

例1 ▶ A woman *whose* husband is dead is called a widow.

[所有格；[先行詞] 人・人以外]

_____

- 目的格の関係代名詞that，which，who(m)は省略できる。

例2 ▶ The movie (*which* [*that*]) I saw yesterday was exciting.

[関係代名詞の省略]

_____

② 先行詞を含む関係代名詞what

- 先行詞を含む関係代名詞whatは，「〜すること [もの]」という意味をもち，whatが導く節は主語・目的語・補語になる。

例3 ▶ *What* you need now is a good rest.
　　　［関係代名詞 what］

　　🐾 whatを用いた慣用表現には, what is called (いわゆる), what is better [worse] (さらによい [悪い] ことには), what A is (今のA), what A was [used to be] (昔のA) などがある。

例4 ▶ She is *what is called* an abstract artist.　［whatを用いた慣用表現］

3　関係副詞

　　🐾 2つの文をつなぐ〈接続詞＋副詞〉の働きを併せもつ関係副詞には, when (「時」を表す語が先行詞), where (「場所」を表す語が先行詞), why (the reasonが先行詞), how (先行詞なし) がある。

例5 ▶ Dolly eats only fruit and vegetables. That was *how* she lost weight.
　　　［関係副詞 how］

4　制限用法・非制限用法

　　🐾 関係代名詞のwho, whose, whom, whichと関係副詞のwhen, whereには, 先行詞を後ろから修飾する「制限用法」と, その前にコンマ [,] を置いて, 先行詞を補足的に説明する「非制限用法」がある。

例6 ▶ He has two daughters *who* have fair hair.　［制限用法］

例7 ▶ He has two daughters, *who* have fair hair.　［非制限用法］

　　🐾 関係代名詞のthat, whatと関係副詞のwhy, howには非制限用法はない。

【自分で飛び回るの!】

🐾 関係代名詞whatには「もの [こと]」という先行詞の意味が含まれているので，その前には先行詞を置かない。

* a bunch of A 「多数のA」

① There's a bunch of bird watchers out today.

_____

② They'll be taking pictures so you should get out and start flying around.

_____

③ That's not exactly what I meant.

_____

LET'S TRY

A カッコ内の適当なものを選んでみよう。

1. 恐竜が絶滅した理由を知っていますか?

   Do you know the reason (how / why) the dinosaurs died out?

2. めったに本を読まない高校生が多い。

   There are many high school students (who / whom) seldom read books.

3. この記事には私には意味のわからない単語がいくつかある。

   There're some words in this article (what / whose) meanings I don't understand.

B 関係詞でカッコを埋めて英文を完成させてみよう。

1. 妹はロンドンへ行って, そこで仕事をみつけた。

   My sister went to London, (   ) she found a job.

2. 私たちは道に迷い, さらに悪いことには雨まで降り出した。

   We lost our way, and (   ) was worse, it started to rain.

3. 1964年は日本で最初にオリンピックが開催された年だ。

   1964 was the year (   ) the Olympic Games were first held in Japan.

C カッコ内の語句を並べかえて, 英文を完成させてみよう。

1. 大切なことは, 何事にも全力を尽くすことだ。(関係代名詞 what)

   What [best / do / everything / important / in / is / is / to / your].

   _____.

2. 私たちはヒースローでタクシーに乗り, ケンジントンで降りた。(get out)

   We [and / at / at / got / got / Heathrow / into / Kensington / out / the taxi].

   _____.

3. 私は時間通りに仕事を始め，夜遅くまで続けた。(start *doing*)

I [and ／ at night ／ kept on ／ on ／ started ／ time ／ until late ／ working ／ working].

_____

_____ .

D 下線部に入る最も適当なものを選んでみよう。

1. Please let me know the date _____ you are available for an interview.

    (A) when   **(B)** where   **(C)** which

2. The north ward is for patients _____ ability to move around is limited.

    (A) who   **(B)** whom   **(C)** whose

3. We installed some expensive equipment, _____ broke down just in two weeks.

    (A) that   **(B)** what   **(C)** which

E 下線部に入る最も適当なものを選んでみよう。

1. All of the hospitals _____ offer foreign language assistance are listed in the booklet.

    (A) what   **(B)** where   **(C)** which   **(D)** whose

2. Every applicant _____ was interviewed will receive a written response within a week.

    (A) which   **(B)** who   **(C)** whom   **(D)** whose

3. The best way to influence others is talk about _____ they want and show them how to get it.

    (A) of which   **(B)** what   **(C)** which   **(D)** whom

Unit 19

比較
COMPARISON

WORDS TO REMEMBER　語群・頭文字をヒントにカッコを埋めてみよう。

（1）　いくつかの　（　　　　　　　　　　　　）

（2）　以前の　（　　　　　　　　　　）

（3）　面白い　（　　　　　　　　　）

（4）　点　（　　　　　　　　　　　）

（5）　ばかげた　（　　　　　　　　　）

（6）　払い戻し　（　　　　　　　　　　）

（7）　一般に　（ g　　　　　　　　　）

（8）　宗教　（ r　　　　　　　　）

（9）　費用　（ e　　　　　　　　）

（10）　面接　（ i　　　　　　　　　）

［語群］

《 funny ／ previous ／ reimbursement ／ ridiculous ／ several ／ way 》

EXPRESSIONS TO REMEMBER　カッコを埋めて英文を完成させてみよう。

1　grow to *do* ／ 〜するようになる

　あなたはこの町が気に入るようになりますよ。

　You'll (　　　　　　　　　　　　　　　　　　　　　　).

2　make an impression on A ／ Aに印象を与える

　マチュピチュは深く彼女の印象に残った。

　Machu Picchu (　　　　　　　　　　　　　　　　　　).

＊ Machu Picchu「マチュピチュ」ペルーにあるインカ帝国の都市遺跡。

3 once... ／ いったん…すれば

太陽が沈むとすぐに涼しくなるでしょう。

(   ), the air will

become cool.

4 tell A B ／ AにBを話す

彼は時々私たちに面白い話をしてくれる。

He (   ).

 GRAMMAR AND USAGE TO REMEMBER 例文を和訳してみよう。

1 原級表現

🐾 2つ以上のものを，その大きさや程度などについて比べる場合，形容詞や副詞の語形を「原級」，「比較級」，「最上級」に変化させて表現する。

🐾 原級表現には，〈as＋原級＋as A〉（Aと同じくらい〜），〈not as [so] ＋原級＋as A〉（Aほど〜でない），〈倍数詞＋as＋原級＋as A〉（Aの…倍〜），〈否定語 (no, nothingなど) ＋as [so] ＋原級＋as A〉（Aほど〜なものはない），〈as many as＋数詞〉（〜もの）などがある。

例1 ▶ Emi speaks French *as fluently as* a native speaker.　［原級表現］

_____

2 比較級表現

🐾 2人の人や2つの物を比較して「AはBより〜である」という場合には，比較級を用いて，〈比較級＋than...〉（…より〜）で表す。

例2 ▶ Women generally live *longer than* men.　［比較級表現］

_____

🐾 そのほかの比較級表現には，〈比較級＋and＋比較級〉（ますます〜；だんだん〜），〈the＋比較級, the＋比較級〉（〜すればするほど，ますます…），〈比較級＋than any other＋A（単数名詞）〉（ほかのどんなAより〜），no later than A（遅くともAまでには）などがある。

🐾 比較級の意味をもつラテン系比較級 *be* superior to A（Aより優れている），*be* senior to A（Aより年上である），*be* preferable to A（Aより好ましい）などはthanの代わりにtoを伴う。

例3 ▶ She thinks that divorce *is preferable to* living with a husband she
no longer loves. ［ラテン系比較級］

🐾 比較級の強調には，much，far，evenを用いる。

③ 最上級表現

🐾 3つ以上のものを比較して「…の中で最も～」という場合には，最上級を用い
て，〈the＋最上級＋of＋複数を表す語句［in＋範囲・場所］〉で表す。

例4 ▶ Mont Blanc is *the highest* mountain *in* the Alps. ［最上級表現］

🐾 そのほかの最上級表現には，〈the＋序数詞＋最上級＋A〉(…番目に～なA)，
〈one of the＋最上級＋複数形の名詞〉(最も～なものの1つ)，at least (少な
くとも)，at *one's* best (最高の状態で)，make the best of A (Aをできるだけ
利用する)，do *one's* best (最善を尽くす) などがある。

例5 ▶ New York is *one of the largest cities* in the world.
［〈one of the＋最上級＋複数形の名詞〉］

🐾 最上級の強調には，by far，veryを用いる。

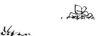

【振り向くのが面倒くさい…】

🐾　moreは「より〜だ」という比較級をつくる記号の役割を果たす。

① If I were you, I'd be totally ashamed to have someone see me sitting around holding a stupid blanket!

_____

_____

② And that dog lying in your lap looks even more ridiculous.

_____

③ I'd bite her, but I'm facing the wrong way.

_____

A カッコ内の適当なものを選んでみよう。

1. トムは私たちのクラスのほかのどの少年よりも背が高い。

   Tom is taller than any other (boy ╱ boys) in our class.

2. 日本の気候はイングランドの気候よりも穏やかである。

   The climate of Japan is milder (than ╱ to) that of England.

3. カリフォルニアはアメリカ合衆国で3番目に大きな州だ。

   California is the third (large ╱ largest) state in the United States.

B 日本文を英語に直してみよう。

1. 君のクラスの中で誰が一番速く走りますか (runner)？

   _____ ?

2. 東京スカイツリーは東京タワーの約2倍の高さ (tall) だ。

   _____ .

3. ヨーロッパでは野球よりサッカーのほうがずっと (much) 人気がある。

   _____ .

C カッコ内の語句を並べかえて，英文を完成させてみよう。

1. もし私があなたなら，このマウンテンバイクは買いません。(if I were you)

   If [bike ╱ buy ╱ I ╱ I ╱ not ╱ this ╱ mountain ╱ were ╱ would ╱ you,].

   _____ .

2. タクシーの運転手に私の荷物を玄関まで運んでもらった。(have A *do*)

   I [baggage ╱ carry ╱ door ╱ driver ╱ had ╱ my ╱ the front ╱ the taxi ╱ to].

   _____ .

3. お恥ずかしいことですが，私はあなたに年齢でうそをつきました。（*be* ashamed to *do*）

    I［ I ／ about ／ am ／ age ／ ashamed ／ lied ／ my ／ say ／ to ／ to ／ that ／ you ］.

    _____

    _____.

D 下線部に入る最も適当なものを選んでみよう。

1. Taking the bus to Los Angeles is _____ than taking the train.

    (A) economical　**(B)** more economical　**(C)** the most economical

2. The new model is superior _____ the previous one in several ways.

    (A) as　**(B)** than　**(C)** to

3. All application forms must be submitted no _____ than 5 o'clock on Monday.

    (A) later　**(B)** latest　**(C)** least

E 下線部に入る最も適当なものを選んでみよう。

1. Hinduism has grown to become the world's _____ largest religion, after Christianity and Islam.

    (A) one-third　**(B)** three　**(C)** third　**(D)** thirdly

2. Reimbursements for travel expenses will be paid as _____ as possible once all the necessary forms are submitted.

    (A) more quickly　**(B)** most quickly

    (C) quickly　**(D)** the most quickly

3. Making a good first impression in an interview is _____ more important than telling the interviewers everything you know about the company.

    (A) by far　**(B)** far　**(C)** too　**(D)** very

Unit 20

否定
NEGATION

LET'S LEARN

WORDS TO REMEMBER 語群・頭文字をヒントにカッコを埋めてみよう。

（1）価値がある　（　　　　　　　　　　　）

（2）主要都市　（　　　　　　　　　　）

（3）南極　（　　　　　　　　）

（4）避難者　（　　　　　　　）

（5）部署　（　　　　　　　）

（6）理想的な　（　　　　　　　　　）

（7）霧　（ f　　　　　　　）

（8）社会　（ s　　　　　　　）

（9）努力　（ e　　　　　　　）

（10）もや　（ m　　　　　　　　）

［語群］

《 Antarctic ／ department ／ evacuee ／ ideal ／ metropolis ／ valuable 》

EXPRESSIONS TO REMEMBER カッコを埋めて英文を完成させてみよう。

1 be wrong with A ／ Aの調子が悪い

この目覚まし時計はどうも調子がよくない。

Something (　　　　　　　　　　　　　　　　　　　　　　　　).

2 bring A B ／ AにBを持ってくる

私に水を一杯持ってきてくれませんか？

Will you (　　　　　　　　　　　　　　　　　　　　　　　　)?

3 ensure that.../…ということを確実にする

必ず新鮮な果物と野菜を十分に食べるようにしなさい。

(   ) plenty of

fresh fruit and vegetables.

4 make an effort／努力する

サリーは日本語をマスターしようと努力した。

Sally (   ).

 GRAMMAR AND USAGE TO REMEMBER 例文を和訳してみよう。

1 否定の表し方

- 🐾 never (一度も〜でない；決して〜でない) は,〈be動詞＋never〉,〈never ＋一般動詞〉,〈助動詞＋never＋一般動詞[be動詞]〉の形で強い否定を表す。

例1 ▶ Vegetarians *never* eat meat. ［強い否定を表すnever］

_____

- 🐾 notは,文全体を否定する場合にはbe動詞・助動詞の後ろにつけ,語句・節 のみを否定する場合には打ち消す語句・節の前に置く。
- 🐾 noは,名詞の前につけて「まったく〜ない」という否定を表す。
- 🐾 noneは,「誰も[何も]〜ない」の意味で人にも物にも用いる。

2 準否定語

- 🐾 弱い否定を表す「準否定語」には,「程度」を表すhardly (ほとんど〜ない), scarcely (ほとんど〜ない),「頻度」を表すseldom (めったに〜ない), rarely (めったに〜ない),弱い否定を表すfew ([数が] ほとんどない), little ([量・程度が] ほとんどない) などがある。

例2 ▶ Snow *seldom* melts in the Antarctic.

［「頻度」を表す準否定語seldom］

_____

- 🐾 a fewは「少しある」,a littleは「いくらかはある」という意味を表す。

3 部分否定

🐾 否定語が，all，always，necessarily，absolutelyなどの語とともに用いられると，not all～（すべて～とは限らない），not always～（いつも～とは限らない），not necessarily～（必ずしも～とは限らない），not absolutely～（完全に～というわけではない）のように100%は否定しない「部分否定」を表す。

例3 ▶ A great player doesn't *necessarily* become a good coach.

［部分否定］

---

4 否定語を用いた否定表現

🐾 否定語を用いた否定表現には，cannot help *doing*（～せずにはいられない），cannot～too C（いくらCしてもしすぎることはない），never [not] ... without *doing*（～すると必ず…する），not～until ...（…して初めて～する），do nothing but *do*（～ばかりしている），not A but B（AではなくてB）などがある。

例4 ▶ In a place like this, you *cannot* be *too* careful.

［否定語を用いた否定表現］

---

5 否定語を用いない否定表現

🐾 否定語を用いない否定表現には，*be* free from A（Aがない），fail to *do*（～できない；～しそこなう），*be* far from *doing*（決して～しない），the last A to *do*（最も～しそうにないA）などがある。

例5 ▶ He would be *the last person to do* such a thing.

［否定語を用いない否定表現］

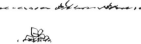

【よくも言ったな!】

🐾 否定語neverは時間の観念を含む語で，基本的には「過去・現在・未来のどの時点をとっても～でない」という意味を表す。

＊ say (that)... 「…であると言う」

＊ not～much of a B 「たいしたBでない」

① Charlie Brown says his elbow hurts so much he may never be able to pitch again.

_____

_____

② Oh, well, he wasn't much of a pitcher anyway.

_____

③　……

A カッコ内の適当なものを選んでみよう。

1. 北極圏の冬では，太陽はいっさい昇ってこない。

   During the Arctic winter, the sun (never / not) rises.

2. ここのコンピューターの全部がインターネットに接続されているわけではない。

   (No / Not) all of these computers are connected to the Internet.

3. 私はオーストラリアの歴史についてほとんど何も知らない。

   I (hardly / seldom) know anything about the history of Australia.

B カッコを埋めて英文を完成させてみよう。

1. 公園にはそのとき子どもたちはほとんどいなかった。

   (　　　　　　) children were in the park at that time.

2. 金持ちや有名人になりたいという願望を全くもっていない人もいる。

   Some people have (　　　　　) desire to be rich or famous.

3. この写真を見ると必ず死んだ叔母のことを思い出す。

   I cannot look at this photo (　　　　　) thinking of my dead aunt.

C カッコ内の語句を並べかえて，英文を完成させてみよう。

1. うまくいくとは思わないけど，とにかくやってみるよ。（副詞 anyway）

   I [anyway / but / don't / I'll / it / work / think / try / will].

   _____.

2. あなたも大人になればお父さんを理解できるようになるよ。(*be* able to *do*)

You [able ／ be ／ father ／ grow ／ to ／ understand ／ up ／ when ／ will ／ you ／ your].

_____

_____.

3. その先生は生徒たちにたいした印象を残さなかった。(not ～ much of a B)

The teacher [an impression ／ didn't ／ make ／ much ／ on ／ of ／ the students].

_____.

D 下線部に入る最も適当なものを選んでみよう。

1. We cannot realize the happiness of school days _____ we work in society.

    (A) if   **(B)** that   **(C)** until

2. My father _____ went on business trips without bringing us some presents.

    (A) never   **(B)** no   **(C)** none

3. Life is valuable not because we have many years _____ because we have only once.

    (A) and   **(B)** but   **(C)** or

E 下線部に入る最も適当なものを選んでみよう。

1. I can't help _____ that the evacuees will be able to return to their homes as soon as possible.

    (A) hope   **(B)** hoped   **(C)** hoping   **(D)** to hope

2. _____ of the network engineers in the department understood what was wrong with the intranet.

    (A) Never   **(B)** No   **(C)** None   **(D)** Not

3. April is very far _____ being an ideal month in London, but the metropolis is free from fog and mist.

    (A) by   **(B)** from   **(C)** on   **(D)** to

 WORDS TO REMEMBER ※括弧内の数字は初出のUNIT番号です。

donor（12）	寄贈者	gauge（7）	～を評価する
due（10）	締切りの	generally（19）	一般に
		generate（11）	～を発生させる
		gorgeous（16）	豪華な
E		guarantee（1）	～を保証する

effective（11）	効果がある		
effort（20）	努力	**H**	
emergency（16）	緊急事態	hamper（1）	かご
environment（7）	環境	harmful（10）	有害な
equipment（18）	装置	heartwarming（5）	心優しい
error（20）	誤り	hike（9）	ハイキング
establish（3）	～を設置する	hometown（8）	故郷
evident（1）	明白な	host（5）	～を開催する
excess（11）	余分な		
exhibit（2）	展示品		
exhibition（3）	展示会	**I**	
expense（19）	費用	ideal（20）	理想的な
expressway（5）	高速道路	ignore（7）	～を無視する
extremely（11）	きわめて	illiterate（4）	読み書きのできない
		impossible（8）	不可能な
		impression（2）	印象
F		inclement（16）	荒れ模様の
facilities（1）	施設	independence（1）	独立
fair（18）	金髪の	individual（17）	個人
faithful（6）	忠実な	influence（18）	～に影響を与える
favorable（2）	良好な	install（18）	～を設置する
figure（3）	人影	interview（19）	面接
fine（14）	罰金		
fix（5）	～を修理する		
flight（2）	便	**K**	
flowerbed（14）	花壇	kindergarten（8）	幼稚園
fog（20）	霧		
fund（4）	基金	**L**	
funny（19）	面白い	latest（14）	最新の
furniture（7）	家具	lightning（15）	稲妻
		linguistics（16）	言語学
G		local（4）	地元の
garage（9）	ガレージ		

M			
major (17)	主要な	property (6)	所有地
manufacture (9)	～を生産する	psychology (16)	心理学
matter (17)	物質	publisher (11)	出版社
methodology (4)	方法論	purchase (7)	～を購入する
metropolis (20)	主要都市		
mist (20)	もや		

Q

quality (7)	品質
questionnaire (7)	アンケート

N

nephew (5)	甥
nervous (8)	不安な
nightfall (2)	夕暮れ
notice (8)	通知
notify (16)	～に知らせる
nutritious (17)	栄養価が高い

R

raise (15)	～を栽培する
reaction (6)	反応
rear (5)	裏の
reduce (9)	～を緩和する
refugee (4)	難民
refuse (3)	～を断る
reject (13)	～を断る
region (6)	地方
registered (13)	正規の
reimbursement (19)	払い戻し
religion (19)	宗教
relocate (14)	移住する
remark (11)	意見
repair (15)	～を修理する
require (13)	～を要求する
resources (6)	資源
resume (10)	履歴書
retirement (14)	退職
reveal (17)	～を漏らす
ridiculous (19)	ばかげた
routinely (8)	日常的に
rude (3)	失礼な
run (15)	流れる

O

observance (16)	守ること
obtain (5)	～を得る
octopus (12)	タコ
offer (18)	～を提供する
organic (17)	有機栽培による
organically (15)	有機的に
origin (3)	起源
overseas (2)	海外で

P

part (15)	部品
passenger (12)	乗客
patient (11)	患者
pirate (11)	海賊
portion (4)	部分
potential (14)	可能性のある
preference (13)	好み
previous (19)	以前の
prompt (9)	時間に正確な

S

safe (18)	金庫

same-day（12）	日帰りの	way（19）	点
scholarship（12）	奨学金	weed（14）	雑草
serious（7）	深刻な	widow（18）	未亡人
several（19）	いくつかの	wise（13）	賢明な
severity（9）	深刻さ		
shot（15）	注射		
shower（1）	夕立		
society（20）	社会		
solution（8）	解決法		
station（9）	局		
stimulating（1）	刺激的な		
structure（3）	構造		
stuffy（8）	息苦しい		
submission（16）	提出		
submit（10）	〜を提出する		
symptom（9）	症状		

T

tentative（10）	仮の
tornado（8）	竜巻
tourist（15）	観光客
traveling（5）	巡回の

U

unpredictable（6）	予測のつかない
urban（14）	都会の

V

valuable（20）	価値がある
variation（9）	変動
vet（17）	獣医
volatile（4）	揮発性の

W

ward（18）	病棟
wastebasket（10）	くずかご

EXPRESSIONS TO REMEMBER

A

ahead of schedule （2）	予定より早く
apply for A （12）	Aを申請する
as C as possible （13）	できるだけCに
as long as... （4）	…さえすれば
as soon as... （4）	…するとすぐに
ask if... （16）	…かどうか尋ねる
at the beginning of A （5）	Aの初めに
at the latest （13）	遅くとも

B

be accompanied by A （17）	Aが付き添っている
be aware of A （17）	Aに気づいている
be delayed （16）	遅れる
be interested in *doing* （2）	～することに興味がある
be kind enough to *do* （9）	親切にも～する
be known for A （9）	Aで知られている
be late for A （13）	Aに遅刻する
be made up of A （16）	Aから成り立っている
be postponed （16）	延期になる
be subject to A （14）	Aを受けやすい
be superior to A （7）	Aより優れている
be wrong with A （20）	Aの調子が悪い
bring A B （20）	AにBを持ってくる
bring A to B （13）	AをBに持って行く
burn down A （15）	Aを焼き尽す
by the time... （5）	…するときまでは

C

C one （17）	Cなもの
change A into B （6）	AをBに変える
contribute A to B （12）	AをBに寄付する

D

donate A to B （4）	AをBに寄付する

E

enable A to *do* （11）	Aが～できるようにする
encourage A to *do* （12）	Aに～するよう推奨する
ensure that... （20）	…ということを確実にする
equip A with B （1）	AにBを装備する

F

finish *doing* （5）	～し終える
fill out A （7）	Aに必要事項を記入する

G

give up A （3）	Aをあきらめる；Aを譲る
go on a trip （4）	旅行に出かける
grow to *do* （19）	～するようになる

H

help A *do* （5）	Aが～するのを手伝う
how to *do* （18）	～の仕方

I

import A from B （11）
　　AをBから輸入する：AをBから導入する
insert A into B （10）　　AをBに挿入する
It is C to *do* （8）　　～することはCだ

K

keep A C （14）　　AをCにしておく

L

leave A C （15）　　AをCの状態にしておく
Let me *do* （18）　　私に～させてください
look down on A （3）　　Aを軽蔑する

M

make A C （8）　　AをCにする
make an effort （20）　　努力する
make an impression on A （19）
　　Aに印象を与える
move into A （3）　　Aに引っ越す
move to A （1）　　Aに引っ越す

N

note that... （10）　　…ということに注意する

O

on time （15）　　時間どおりに
once... （19）　　いったん…すれば
out of stock （15）　　品切れで

P

plan to *do* （6）　　～する予定である
pretend to *do* （3）　　～するふりをする
prove to be C （11）　　Cであることがわかる
provide A for B （9）　　AをBに供給する
provide A with B （6）　　AにBを提供する

R

reserve A for B （12）
　　AをBのために予約する
retire from A （1）　　Aを退職する

S

say that... （6）　　…と書いてある
see how... （9）　どのように…かを観察する
sell A to B （11）　　AをBに売る
send A to B （14）　　AをBに送る
show A B （18）　　AにBを教える
so C that... （8）　　とてもCなので…
so that A can *do* （7）　Aが～できるように
suggest *doing* （8）　　～することを提案する

T

talk about A （18）　　Aについて話す
tell A B （19）　　AにBを話す
tell A of B （1）　　AにBについて話す
thanks to A （2）　　Aのおかげで
the cost of A （17）　　Aの値段
those who～ （14）　　～する人々
too C for A to *do* （7）
　　Aが～するにはCすぎる

W

without notice （10）　　予告なしに
without permission （10）　　許可なく
would like to *do* （2）　　～したい

LET'S READ

, so... （6）

 **LET'S READ** 和訳して質問に答えてみよう。

 **Unit 1**

My favorite dance company performed in town last weekend. Apparently, tickets sold out fast. I wasn't able to get any tickets, and felt disappointed. But on the night before the show, my friend called me. Her brother was a dancer in the show, and had given her two VIP tickets. She kindly invited me, so we went together. The dance performance was beautiful. My friend's brother was such a wonderful dancer, too. After the show, my friend asked if I would like to go backstage to meet her brother and the other dancers. Of course, I said yes!

＊ apparently「どうも」　＊ sell out「売り切れる」　＊ the night before A「Aの前の晩に」

●QUESTION●

How was the performance?

　　　　(A) beautiful　　**(B)** disappointing　　**(C)** wonderful

 **Unit 2**

The music of Ludwig van Beethoven is well-known throughout the world. The composer learned to play the piano from an early age. His father taught him as a child but the lessons were very strict. Sometimes practice was so hard that the young Beethoven cried. However his father knew that Beethoven's musical talent was superb. Beethoven composed many masterpieces. Even when he suffered from hearing loss, he continued to make music. In Beethoven's time, audiences often thought his music difficult to understand. But today, over 200 years later, Beethoven's music is loved and respected by many people.

＊ Ludwig van Beethoven「ルートヴィヒ・ヴァン・ベートーヴェン」ドイツの作曲家。

＊ think A C「AをCとみなす」　＊ in A's time「Aの時代には」

(5) **●QUESTION●**

When Beethoven suffered from hearing loss what did he do?

    (A) He composed many masterpieces.

    (B) He continued making music.

    (C) He learned to play the piano.

(6)  **Unit 3**

On weekdays I wake up early for work. I need to catch a rush-hour train to get to the office on time. The other day, when I got on the train it was empty. This was a surprise, but I didn't think much about it. When I got off the train I popped into a café to grab a coffee, then carried it on my way to the office. I arrived at my usual time but the building was locked. First I panicked, but when I calmed down I realized it was the weekend! I could have slept in!

    ＊ pop into A「Aにちょっと立ち寄る」   ＊ grab a coffee「コーヒーを急いで飲む」
    ＊ sleep in「朝寝坊する（＝sleep late）」

(7) **●QUESTION●**

Where did the author pop into after getting off the train?

    (A) a café   **(B)** the building   **(C)** the office

(8)  **Unit 4**

Last summer I went traveling by myself for the first time. Before, I always went on vacation with family or friends. But I wanted to explore somewhere on my own. The trip lasted three weeks. It was a big adventure for me. I was nervous at first. But I enjoyed my trip a lot! I visited seven cities in four countries and went hiking up a mountain. It was exciting to meet people from all over the world. I made new friends and learned about different cultures. Traveling solo has made me more confident. Now I am planning my next trip. I want to travel more.

＊ by oneself「ひとりで(=on one's own／solo)」

(9)  ●QUESTION●

What was the trip like?

    (A) A big adventure

    (B) A hike up a mountain

    (C) My next trip

(10) **Unit 5**

    The Peanuts comics have been adored by people of all ages since 1950. Its author Charles Schulz was able to captivate audiences all over the world. Many of the characters that appeared in the comics were drawn from the author's own life. In fact Charlie Brown, the main character, was based on the author himself. Apparently, Schulz was shy and nervous as a child, just like Charlie Brown. Schulz also used to have a dog. It wasn't a beagle, but looked like Snoopy. Peanuts portrayed the complex lives of children with humor and tenderness. They are popular to this day.

    ＊ adore A「Aが大好きである」 ＊ of all ages「あらゆる年代の」
    ＊ draw from A「Aから引き出す」

(11)  ●QUESTION●

Which character was based on the author himself?

    (A) Charlie Brown   **(B)** Charles Schulz   **(C)** Snoopy

(12) **Unit 6**

    It was the middle of a long and cold winter in New York. There was snow everywhere. I was taking a walk in Central Park and some kids were building snowmen and having snowball fights. Suddenly, a big snowball hit me in the face. "Ouch!" I shouted. When I looked to see who threw it, I couldn't believe my eyes. It was my friend from high school whom I hadn't seen in over 10 years! My friend smiled and explained, "I saw you from a distance and recognized you right away!" I laughed and said, "Ha! You were always good at baseball."

* snowball fight 「雪合戦」　* right away 「すぐに」

(13) ● QUESTION ●

What hit the author in the face?

        (A) A ball   **(B)** A snowball   **(C)** A snowman

(14)  **Unit 7**

"Excuse me, may I check your bag?" asked the security officer.

"Go ahead," replied the young man.

The officer then said, "Could you please open it?"

"Yes, of course," answered the man.

Inside the bag there was an apple, a chocolate bar and a black case. The officer looked suspiciously at the case. She requested the man to get the case out and open it.

The young man sighed. "Oh, that? Here you are," he said and opened it. It was his packed lunch. "I made these sandwiches in the morning," he said.

"Well, you'd better put them away before someone else eats them!" The officer laughed, and let him go.

* request A to *do* 「Aに〜するよう頼む」　* packed lunch 「お弁当」
* put A away 「Aをしまう」

(15) ● QUESTION ●

What was in his packed lunch?

        (A) A chocolate bar   **(B)** An apple   **(C)** Sandwiches

⑯

It was the beginning of spring break. Molly and Frankie went outside to play in the park across the road. Some older kids were playing catch. By the swings, a group of young children were drawing with sticks in the sand. Frankie got out his yellow kite. Suddenly, a gust of wind whisked the kite out of his hands. The kite got blown away. He was very upset. But Molly noticed the kite was stuck up a tree near the see-saw. She climbed the tree. Within a few minutes Molly brought the kite down. Frankie was so happy he cheered!

* gust of wind「突風」　　* get blown away「飛ばされる」

⑰ ●QUESTION●

Where were the young children drawing?

    (A) Across the road

    (B) By the swings

    (C) Near the see-saw

⑱

Rosa Parks is widely recognized in America as the "mother of the modern day civil rights movement." On December 1 1955, Parks refused to surrender her seat to a white male passenger on a bus in Montgomery, Alabama. For this, she was arrested by the police. This led to a boycott of the city bus line. Martin Luther King Jr. became the spokesperson of the Bus Boycott, and talked of the importance of nonviolence. The boycott continued for over a year. Thousands of people took part to demand equal rights to all people. Rosa Parks strongly believed in racial equality, and her courage and determination changed the country.

* Rosa Parks 「ローザ・パークス」アメリカ公民権運動指導者。アラバマ州モンゴメリーの黒人差別バスに抗議し乗車拒否運動を起こした。

* civil rights movement「公民権運動」

＊Martin Luther King Jr. 「マーティン・ルーサー・キング・ジュニア」アメリカの牧師・黒人公民権運動の指導者。

＊talk of A 「について話す」　＊nonviolence 「非暴力」

＊lead to A 「Aにつながる」　＊believe in A 「Aを正しいと信じる」

(19) ●QUESTION●

Who did Rosa Parks refuse to surrender her seat to?

(A) A white male passenger

(B) The police

(C) The spokesperson

(20)  Unit 10

"Rosie, could you do me a favor?"

"Oh, how can I help you, Janelle?"

"Well, my cousin Chris is visiting from LA next Tuesday. His plane arrives at 2 pm and he needs a ride from the airport. But I must be at a meeting all afternoon. Would it be possible for you to drive to the airport and meet him?"

"Sure, Janelle. I have an appointment in the morning but should be finished by noon."

"Thank you so much, Rosie!"

"But just in case there are any delays, could I have your cousin's phone number?"

"Of course. I shall give you his contact details right away."

＊just in case... 「…の場合に備えて」　＊contact detail 「連絡先」

(21) ●QUESTION●

When will the plane arrive?

(A) All afternoon　　**(B)** At 2 pm　　**(C)** In the morning

(22)

I always have a hard time studying for exams. It's difficult to concentrate on my own. But funny enough, I can focus on my studies when I am with other people. So, I suggested to some of my friends to come to my house so we could study together. Most of my friends seemed happier studying on their own. But luckily there were two who were interested. So, we got together and did some revision at home. Time flew by and we got so much work done! A few weeks ago we took our exams. I received my results today. Guess what? I got the best grades in school.

＊fly by「飛ぶように過ぎる」　＊get A done「Aを〜させる」　＊Guess what?「どうだったと思う？」

(23) ●QUESTION●

What did the author receive today?

  (A) Exams **(B)** Results **(C)** Revision

(24)

I do all my grocery-shopping at the farmers' market held every Friday and Saturday. All of the produce sold there is grown and prepared on urban farms in Portland. The farmers' market began over 30 years ago and has been a favorite among locals since the beginning. Fruit and vegetables can be bought by weight, and the cheese stall not only serves the best cheese but good yoghurt is also sold. At the bakers' stall, you can have sandwiches made on the spot. Once, I was even given a slice of cake for free. "It's my birthday today, so it's on me!" the baker said. The gesture made me very happy.

＊urban farm「都市農場」　＊Portland「ポートランド」アメリカ・オレゴン州北西部の都市。
＊on the spot「その場で」　＊be on A「Aのおごりだ」

(25) ●QUESTION●

What was given for free?

(A) A slice of cake   **(B)** Sandwiches   **(C)** The best cheese

(26)  Unit 13

My friend Dinah had just come back from studying in Spain for two years, so we decided to meet for dinner. We booked a table for seven o'clock. She was already waiting for me at the table when I arrived at the restaurant. I sat down and we got to talking straight away. There was so much catching up to do. After some time the waiter came to take our order, but we had to apologize. We were so busy talking that we hadn't even looked at the menu on the table! The waiter laughed and said, "OK, I'll come back in five minutes!"

* get *doing*「〜し始める」　 * straight away「すぐに (=at once)」
* catching up「久しぶりの話」

(27) ●QUESTION●

When did the waiter come to the table?

(A) After some time

(B) At seven o'clock

(C) In five minutes

(28)  Unit 14

My brother and I are identical twins. We look alike but have completely different personalities. I can be slow at making decisions but he is always quick to decide. He loses patience when I can't choose what to order on the menu, which is understandable. There is only so much waiting you can do when you're hungry! I get frustrated with him too. He leaps into action then just as quickly regrets it. Once, we were meeting up after work to go to the theater. He was running late and needed to catch a train. Without thinking, he jumped onto the nearest train, but as the doors shut he realized he was on an express train going the opposite direction. We were lucky we made it to the show on time!

* identical 「一卵性双生児の」　* leap into action 「慌てて行動する」
* meet up 「待ち合わせて会う」　* *be* running late 「（予定より）遅れている」
* make it to A 「Aに間に合う」

(29)

When were they meeting up?

　　　　(A) After work　　**(B)** On time　　**(C)** When catching a train

(30)

　　　　See the photograph hanging on the wall? That's me sleeping on the grass hugging my security blanket. I must have been about three years old. The blanket was made for me by my aunt. It was basically like my best friend. I took the blanket everywhere with me. In the park you could tell straight away where I was, because I was the little running kid with the ragged blanket tucked into the neck of my tee-shirt. With my blanket I felt like a super hero. But over the years, it became more worn out, until finally there was only a small corner of it left. It's there framed on the wall next to the photo of me!

* security blanket 「安心毛布」安心感を得るために子どもがいつも抱きしめている毛布・ぬいぐるみなど。
* worn out「すり切れた」

(31) **●QUESTION●**

What did the author feel like with the blanket?

　　　　(A) A super hero　　**(B)** My best friend　　**(C)** My tee-shirt

(32) Unit 16

　　　　The Woodstock Music and Art Fair, also simply known as "Woodstock," was held in the summer of 1969 and is one of the most famous rock music festivals of the era. It took place on a large dairy farm in Bethel, New York, and was billed as "Three Days of Peace and Music." Woodstock attracted thousands of people from near and far, which caused long traffic jams between the festival site and the surrounding main roads. Many famous musicians performed there. The performances were held outside, sometimes under rainy weather. The rain made the site very muddy but it didn't stop the crowds from enjoying the festival.

* simply known as A「短縮してＡと知られている」
* Bethel「ベテル」ウッドストック・フェスティバルが開催されたニューヨーク州サリバン郡の農村部。
* from near and far「近隣だけでなく遠方からも」

(33) ●QUESTION●

Where was Woodstock held?

      (A) On a cattle farm   **(B)** On a dairy farm   **(C)** On a fruit farm

(34)

      Immediately after the birth of his child, Luke took paternity leave so that he could spend time with his partner Kim and their newborn daughter. As the first few days since childbirth went by, the couple got to know their firstborn and each other better, as partners and as a family. Although it took the new mother and father a while to decide on a name, after a week they were able to register the birth of baby Lily. Kim glowed and said, "We named her Lily, because she bloomed into our lives." Luke added, "And Kim is the most amazing woman. I really hope I can be as good a father as she is a mother."

* paternity leave「夫の育児休暇」   * resister the birth of baby「出生届を出す」

(35) ●QUESTION●

When did they register the baby's birth?

      (A) After a week   **(B)** Immediately after the birth

      (C) The first few days

(36)

It was stormy last night, but when I woke up this morning the sky had cleared. It was such a beautiful day that I was convinced I would not need an umbrella, so I went out with my sunglasses on and left my umbrella. But before I realized, the sky turned dark again. What I should have brought was my umbrella, not my sunglasses! The rain started to pour, which soaked me through. I felt miserable. But after several minutes, the sun came out again and I got to see the biggest rainbow in the sky! This brightened up my day.

＊ brighten up A 「Aを明るくする」

(37) ●QUESTION●

What did the author leave behind this morning?

　　　(A) Dry clothes　　　**(B)** Sunglasses　　　**(C)** Umbrella

(38)

Winter vacation started yesterday. It's the holiday season so we eat more than any other time of year! Our homework this vacation is to bake something special for the family. I don't know if I would ever be able to bake bread better than my mom. My dad bakes the best cookies too, so I don't think I should make any of those. But my parents never make pies. My family loves pumpkin pie so I think that's what I'll make. Tomorrow I am going to the library to look at some recipe books. I hope I can find a good recipe!

＊ holiday season 「年末年始の休暇」

(39) ●QUESTION●

What does the author dad bake best?

　　　(A) Bread　　　**(B)** Cookies　　　**(C)** Pumpkin pie

   My colleague Lana is never late for work. So when she didn't turn up yesterday, I was surprised. No one had heard from her. I called her cell phone, but there was no answer. This got me worried, but after some time she called back. I asked, "Are you OK, Lana?" She replied, "Sorry for not getting in touch. An old lady fell over on the sidewalk, so I called an ambulance. The lady didn't want to be left alone, and asked me to go to the hospital with her. I couldn't refuse. She's fine now. I'll make my way soon. It shouldn't take long from the hospital to the office." I replied, "Lana, there's no need for that. You shouldn't have to think about work now. You deserve a day off!"

   * fall over 「転ぶ」

●QUESTION●

Who went to the hospital?

    (A) Lana   **(B)** The old lady   **(C)** The old lady and Lana

スヌーピーと学ぶ英文法と表現・読解

| 検印省略 | © 2020 年 1 月 31 日　初 版 発 行 |

編著者　　　　　　　　　小 中　　秀 彦

発行者　　　　　　　　　原　　　雅 久
発行所　　　　　　　　株式会社 朝 日 出 版 社
101-0065　東京都千代田区西神田 3-3-5
電話　03-3239-0271〜72
FAX　03-3239-0479
e-mail　text-e@asahipress.com
振替口座　00140-2-46008
組版／ease　製版／錦明印刷